At Least This Place Sells T-Shirts

Other FoxTrot Books by Bill Amend

FoxTrot
Pass the Loot
Black Bart Says Draw
Eight Yards, Down and Out
Bury My Heart at Fun-Fun Mountain
Say Hello to Cactus Flats
May the Force Be With Us, Please
Take Us to Your Mall
The Return of the Lone Iguana

Anthologies

FoxTrot: The Works
FoxTrot *en masse*
Enormously FoxTrot
Wildly FoxTrot

FoxTrot is distributed internationally by Universal Press Syndicate.

At Least This Place Sells T-Shirts copyright © 1996 by Bill Amend. All rights reserved. Printed in the United States of America. No part of this book may be used or reproduced in any manner whatsoever without written permission except in the case of reprints in the context of reviews. For information write Andrews and McMeel, a Universal Press Syndicate Company, 4520 Main Street, Kansas City, Missouri 64111.

ISBN: 0-8362-2120-6

Library of Congress Catalog Card Number: 96-84102

At Least This Place Sells T-Shirts

A FoxTrot Collection
by Bill Amend

Andrews and McMeel
A Universal Press Syndicate Company
Kansas City

To William IV

A LITTLE BACON...
A LITTLE LETTUCE...
A LITTLE TOMATO...

A LITTLE LETTUCE...
A LITTLE TOMATO...
A LITTLE MORE BACON...

A LITTLE MORE TOMATO...
A LITTLE MORE BACON...
A BIT MORE LETTUCE...

A BLTLTBTBLTLB. WHY?

YOU KNOW, PETER, THERE WAS A TIME IN MY LIFE WHEN TRIPS TO THE GROCER TOOK LESS THAN FOUR HOURS.

HI. TWO ADULTS TO SEE "DIE HARD III."

TICKETS || TICKE[

YOU'D THINK THEY'D AT LEAST ASK FOR I.D. BEFORE BOUNCING US.

I JUST LOVE THE SERVICE AT THIS PLACE.

IT'S ENOUGH TO MAKE ME WANT TO EAT LUNCH HERE EVERY DAY.

PAIGE, THE SERVICE HERE STINKS. IT'S THE SLOWEST IN THE WORLD.

EXACTLY.

WHERE CAN PAIGE BE?! SHE'S BEEN GONE FOR TWO HOURS!

WILL YOU QUIT PACING AROUND?!

5

FoxTrot
BILL AMEND

PAIGE, DO YOU REMEMBER MARGARET O'DELL FROM MY BOOK CLUB?

THE WEIRD, PREGNANT LADY?

WELL, SHE'S NO LONGER PREGNANT. SHE WANTED TO KNOW IF YOU COULD BABY-SIT FOR HER TOMORROW NIGHT.

HOW OLD'S THE KID?

HER DAUGHTER'S NINE MONTHS. SHE ALSO WANTED TO KNOW HOW MUCH YOU CHARGE.

LET'S SEE.. NINE MONTHS IS 15 MONTHS UNDER TWO YEARS, INVERT THAT, ADD ONE AND MULTIPLY BY THE BASE RATE.

YOU KNOW, FOR SOMEONE WHO CLAIMS A "B-" IS THE BEST SHE CAN DO IN MATH...

...DIVIDE BY THE GIRL COEFFICIENT OF 1.05, ADD 50 CENTS FOR SHORT NOTICE, ROUND TO TWO DECIMAL PLACES.

HI, THERE! YOU MUST BE LITTLE KATHERINE!

UM, IT'S "KATHERINE" WITH A "K."

THAT'S WHAT I SAID.

NO, YOU SAID "CATHERINE" WITH A "C." I COULD TELL.

HOLD ON — I'LL BE RIGHT BACK.

HI, THERE! YOU MUST BE THE LITTLE GIRL WHO'S GOING TO NEED MASSIVE THERAPY IN 12 YEARS!

OK, THE VIDEO CAMERA I HID IN THIS DOLL SHOULD PROVE I'M RIGHT...

OK, PAIGE, HERE ARE MY GROUND RULES...

IF THERE'S AN ACCIDENT, I WANT YOU TO CALL ME. IF SHE EATS SOMETHING SHE SHOULDN'T, I WANT YOU TO CALL ME. IF SHE CRIES FOR MORE THAN A MINUTE, I WANT YOU TO CALL ME. IF SHE SNEEZES, I WANT YOU TO CALL ME. IF SHE WETS HER DIAPER, I WANT YOU TO CALL ME. IF SHE **DOESN'T** WET HER DIAPER, I WANT YOU TO CALL ME.

THE REST ARE ON THIS LIST.

OOPS! I ALMOST FORGOT—HERE'S THE NUMBER WHERE I'LL BE.

DANG.

PAG!

DID YOU JUST SAY "PAIGE"?!

PAG!

YOU DID! YOU SAID MY NAME!

KATIE, SWEETIE, YOU'RE SO CUTE! I CAN'T BELIEVE YOU SAID MY NAME! THIS IS SOMETHING I'LL NEVER FORGET!

PAG!

...NOT THAT I WON'T **TRY** TO.

KATIE, IT'S PAST YOUR BEDTIME. LET'S GO.

COME ON, KIDDO. TIME FOR SLEEP.

LET ME EXPLAIN SOMETHING TO YOU, YOUNG LADY. BEDTIMES EXIST FOR A REASON. IF YOUR MOTHER WANTS YOU IN BED AT 9:00, YOU GO TO BED AT 9:00. NO "IFS," "ANDS" OR "BUTS." GOT IT?

WAAAA... ZZZZ...

AH, THE HYPOCRISY OF IT ALL...

HOW WAS BABY-SITTING?

AWFUL.

STRESSFUL. MISERABLE. EXHAUSTING.

I TAKE IT IT PAID WELL.

HOW'D YOU KNOW?

FoxTrot
BILL AMEND

12

FoxTrot
BILL AMEND

QUINCY, WHAT IS THIS?!

I LEAVE YOU ALONE FOR TWO MINUTES AND YOU CHEW UP THE COVER OF PAIGE'S FAVORITE FASHION MAGAZINE?!

I EXPECT BETTER OF YOU, QUINCE, I REALLY DO!

OBVIOUSLY, I'VE FAILED TO TRAIN YOU PROPERLY.

THIS IS NOT GOOD.

I'VE TOLD YOU OVER AND OVER TO GO FOR THE **CONTENTS** FIRST!

YOU KNOW, JASON, MOST PEOPLE TRY TO **AVOID** WEARING A BODY CAST IN THE SUMMER.

UGGH.

HI, HONEY. HOW WAS WORK?

VERY, VERY, VERY STRESSFUL.

I'M SORRY.

WHY DO YOU LET JASON CALL ME?

RELAX— I CONFISCATED HIS LAUNCH PAD.

DAD, TALK SOME SENSE INTO MOM.

JASON, WHAT DID YOU DO WITH ALL THOSE EARTHWORMS YOU DUG UP YESTERDAY?

I PUT THEM IN DIRT.

AND WHAT DID YOU DO WITH THE DIRT?

I PUT IT IN A CAN.

WHAT SORT OF CAN?

I THINK IT WAS A COFFEE CAN.

MYSTERY SOLVED, ROGER.

WHAT'S YOUR FORTUNE COOKIE SAY?

"YOU ARE ONE WHO TAKES GREAT CHANCES."

"...AND YOUR SISTER HAS A MAJOR CRUSH ON SOME BOY NAMED JIMMY HANLEY."

DID EVERYONE HEAR THAT?

THAT FIRST PART SURE WAS TRUE. (URP) I WISH WE'D READ FORTUNES **BEFORE** EATING.

FoxTrot
BILL AMEND

HI. WE'D LIKE—...

I KNOW, I KNOW, TWO TICKETS TO "APOLLO 13."

AND NO, WE HAVEN'T GOTTEN A NEW SHIPMENT OF THE "GENE KRANZ" COLLECTOR'S CUPS, AND YES, THERE ARE STILL SEATS AVAILABLE IN THE FRONT ROW.

TICKETS

TICKETS

DO YOU GET THE SENSE THAT WE'VE DONE THIS ONCE TOO OFTEN?

THIS POP-CORN TASTES SALTIER THAN THIS MORNING'S

MOM, CAN I SLEEP OVER AT NICOLE'S HOUSE TONIGHT?

PAIGE, YOU SLEPT OVER THERE LAST NIGHT.

...AND THE THREE NIGHTS BEFORE THAT, AS I RECALL.

WHAT'S WRONG WITH OCCASIONALLY SPENDING A NIGHT HERE AT HOME?

PRESENTING EXHIBITS A, B, C, D AND E.

WE'VE REALLY GOT TO FIND YOUR BROTHER A NEW HOBBY.

MOM, DUCK...

WHAT DO YOU THINK OF MY NEW SUNGLASSES?

ICK.

WHAT DO YOU THINK OF MY NEW SUNGLASSES?

SURELY YOU JEST.

WHAT DO YOU THINK OF MY NEW SUNGLASSES?

THOSE ARE THE SILLIEST LOOKING THINGS I'VE EVER SEEN.

FINALLY, A PAIR NO ONE WILL BORROW.

HEY, DON'T BLAME ME — BLAME BERNOULLI.

NEXT, ON THE CBS EVENING NEWS...

I'VE REALLY GOT TO GET MY ALARM CLOCK FIXED.

WHERE HAVE YOU BEEN ALL DAY?

THERE'S ONLY ONE BIG DRAWBACK TO QUINCY'S PLASTIC IGUANA BALL.

ROLL ROLL ROLL ROLL

ROLL ROLL ROLL

AAAA!

PAIGE KNOWS SOCCER.

FoxTrot
BILL AMEND

WHAT'S WITH ALL THE MASKING TAPE?

MARCUS AND I ARE BUILDING A KITE OUT OF NEWSPAPER AND STICKS.

HERE'S THE CLASSIFIED SECTION — YOU CAN USE IT IF YOU WANT.

THAT'S OK. WE'VE GOT ABOUT 15 GROCERY BAGS FULL OF NEWSPAPERS OUT IN THE GARAGE.

OH, WHAT THE HECK — BETTER SAFE THAN SORRY.

JASON, JUST HOW BIG A KITE ARE YOU PLANNING TO **MAKE**?!

BY THE WAY, IF THE SUN SHOULD APPEAR TO BE BLOCKED OUT FOR LONG PERIODS THIS AFTERNOON...

SO WHAT DO YOU THINK?

I MUST SAY I'M RELIEVED.

WHEN YOU SAID YOU WERE PLANNING TO MAKE A BIG KITE OUT OF NEWSPAPER, I FEARED YOU'D GO OVERBOARD AS YOU USUALLY DO. THIS IS A WELCOME CHANGE, JASON.

I THINK YOUR KITE IS WONDERFUL.

I DIDN'T HAVE THE HEART TO TELL HER THIS IS ONLY A 1/10-SCALE MODEL.

MAYBE WE SHOULD BUILD THE WIND TUNNEL AT MY HOUSE.

WHAT DO YOU THINK OF OUR KITE? WE MADE IT OUT OF OLD NEWSPAPERS.

HEE HEE HEE...

HEH HEH HEH...

WAAA HA HA HA HA HA HA HA HA HA!

HE MUST BE LOOKING AT THE SIDE WITH THE COMICS PAGE.

(SNIFF) PAIGE, COME SEE THIS!

YOU KNOW HOW IN "PEANUTS," POOR, PATHETIC CHARLIE BROWN'S KITE ALWAYS ENDS UP TANGLED IN SOME TREE?

YEAH, SO?

AT LEAST HE GETS **HIS** OFF THE **GROUND**.

GIVE US A BREAK— WE'VE ONLY BEEN AT THIS TWO HOURS!

MAYBE I SHOULD TRY RUNNING OFF THAT LEDGE OVER THERE.

THERE'S GOT TO BE A WAY TO GET THIS KITE AIRBORNE...

WE COULD TRY RUNNING FASTER... WE COULD PRAY FOR MORE WIND... WE COULD TINKER WITH THE DESIGN...

OR...

TOYS + MORE TOYS

DO YOU GET THE SENSE WE'RE ABOUT TO STRADDLE THE LINE BETWEEN GENIUS AND IDIOCY?

NOW, REMEMBER, WE HAVE TO TAPE THESE ON TIGHTLY.

ROCKET ENGINES

ROCKET ENGINES

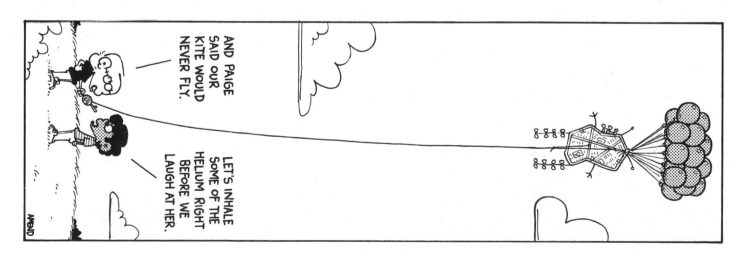

AND PAIGE SAID OUR KITE WOULD NEVER FLY.

LET'S INHALE SOME OF THE HELIUM RIGHT BEFORE WE LAUGH AT HER.

FoxTrot
BILL AMEND

WANNA SEE A FOOLPROOF MAGIC TRICK?

OK.

PICK A CARD. ANY CARD.

MY PSYCHIC POWERS ARE TELLING ME SOMETHING... THEY ARE TELLING ME THAT THE CARD YOU PICKED IS... A CARD **OTHER** THAN THE FOUR OF CLUBS.

UM, THAT'S TRUE.

♪ TA DA! HERE — I'LL DO IT AGAIN. PICK ANOTHER CARD.

ISN'T THIS THE DECK THAT'S **MISSING** THE FOUR OF CLUBS?

WHAT ARE YOU BOYS **DOING**?!

WE FIGURED IF WE DUG A HOLE ALL THE WAY THROUGH THE EARTH'S CRUST, WE'D BE ABLE TO CREATE OUR OWN BACKYARD VOLCANO.

BY THE WAY, DAD MIGHT WANT TO BUY SOME NEW DRILL BITS.

FIRST SHE TELLS US TO PLAY **OUTSIDE**... THEN SHE TELLS US TO PLAY **INSIDE**... THEN SHE TELLS US TO PLAY **OUTSIDE**... THEN SHE TELLS US TO PLAY **INSIDE**...

I THINK HER MISTAKE LIES IN TELLING US TO **PLAY**.

(Beep) WELCOME TO THE COMPUNET GALAXY OF ONLINE SERVICES.

UPGRADING PERIODICALS ARTWORK — PLEASE WAIT...

UPGRADING SPORTS ARTWORK — PLEASE WAIT...

UPGRADING TRAVEL ARTWORK — PLEASE WAIT...

UPGRADING MAILBOX ARTWORK — PLEASE WAIT...

HOW CONVENIENT THAT THEY CHARGE BY THE HOUR.

UPGRADING PERIODICALS ARTWORK UPGRADE — PLEASE WAIT...

HELLO, IS THIS "LARRY KING LIVE"? AM I REALLY ON THE AIR?

YES, YOU ARE, CALLER. DO YOU HAVE A QUESTION FOR THE VICE PRESIDENT?

I CAN'T BELIEVE I GOT THROUGH! I CAN'T BELIEVE WHAT A PRIVILEGE THIS IS! A PERSON COULD WAIT HIS WHOLE LIFE FOR AN OPPORTUNITY LIKE THIS!

CALLER, WHAT'S YOUR QUESTION?

ARE EITHER OF YOUR REFRIGERATORS RUNNING?...

AND PEOPLE THINK **APOLLO 13** HAD A ROUGH FLIGHT.

UM, HOUSTON, WE HAVE ANOTHER PROBLEM...

WANT TO BE THE FIRST TO TRY ONE OF MY BROWNIES?

NO, THANKS.

WANT TO BE THE FIRST TO TRY ONE OF MY BROWNIES?

NO, THANKS.

I GUESS THAT LEAVES ME.

ARE YOU **SURE** YOU DON'T WANT TO BE THE FIRST TO TRY ONE OF MY BROWNIES?

PAIGE, I COULD SMELL THEM BAKING FOR THE LAST FIVE HOURS.

FoxTrot
BILL AMEND

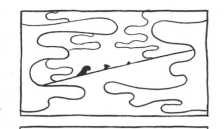

Three silhouettes slowly climb a hill.

A squirrel runs for cover.

First we see a Terminator robot.

Soon he is joined by an Alien.

And a Tyrannosaurus rex.

Together they move in on their unsuspecting prey.

Cut to: Paige Fox picking flowers.

Begin musical number.

FoxTrot

BILL AMEND

ANDY, C'MON! THE KIDS ARE WAITING FOR US OUT IN THE CAR!

I'M NOT FINISHED PACKING!

WELL, HURRY UP! WE'RE GONNA MISS OUR FLIGHT!

I'M DOING THIS AS FAST AS I CAN!

ANDY, LET ME EXPLAIN THE SITUATION...

IF YOU'RE NOT READY IN TWO MINUTES, THE KIDS AND I ARE GOING TO FUN-FUN UNIVERSE WITHOUT YOU.

PROMISE?

MY VOLUME CONTROL DOESN'T SEEM TO WORK.

YOURS IS ON **THIS** ARMREST.

HERE ARE YOUR ROOM KEYS. THE ELEVATORS ARE JUST PAST THE SOUVENIR SHOPS.

GREAT. THANK YOU.

REGISTRATION

WILL YOU BE NEEDING A BELLHOP FOR YOUR BAGS?

THAT'S OK. I THINK WE CAN MANAGE.

REGISTRATION

OOPS, I ALMOST FORGOT— HERE ARE SOME BROCHURES HIGHLIGHTING SOME OF THE MANY WONDERFUL WAYS YOU AND YOUR FAMILY CAN SPEND MONEY WHILE HERE AT FUN-FUN UNIVERSE.

ANYTHING ELSE?

UM, ABOUT THAT BELLHOP...

REGISTRATION

ISN'T THIS HOTEL TERRIFIC, ANDY?

HAIR DRYERS...IRONING BOARDS... A NEWSPAPER EACH MORNING... THEY'LL EVEN DELIVER A PIZZA RIGHT TO YOUR ROOM!

IT'S JUST LIKE BEING AT HOME!

...FOR ONLY $200 A DAY.

CHECK IT OUT— FREE ICE!

MOM, THIS HOTEL IS GREAT!

I'M GLAD YOU LIKE IT.

OUR ROOM CAME STOCKED WITH ALL SORTS OF CANDY BARS AND SODAS. A VERY NICE TOUCH.

REALLY? OURS DIDN'T.

DID YOU LOOK IN THAT LITTLE REFRIGERATOR OVER THERE?

JASON, THAT'S THE MINI-BAR!

THE 20-INCH SNICKERS BARS WERE A TAD STALE, BUT OTHERWISE...

LET THE BANKRUPTCY BEGIN.

GUESS WHAT?! THE GIFT SHOPS LET YOU CHARGE THINGS TO YOUR ROOM!

I'M GONNA TAKE THE UNIRAIL OVER TO THE AMUSEMENT PARK.

I'M GONNA TAKE THE GLASS-BOTTOMED BOAT OVER TO THE AMUSEMENT PARK.

I'M GONNA TAKE THE SKY-TUBE OVER TO THE AMUSEMENT PARK.

ISN'T IT WONDERFUL TO VACATION ALL TOGETHER AS A FAMILY?

I'M GONNA JUST STAY HERE AT THE HOTEL.

28

FoxTrot
BILL AMEND

FoxTrot
BILL AMEND

I'M SO PSYCHED! I GOT THE BEST CLASS SCHEDULE!

OH?

I GOT INTO FIFTH PERIOD TRIGONOMETRY.

WHAT'S SO SPECIAL ABOUT THAT?

FIFTH PERIOD IS RIGHT AFTER LUNCH. IT'S THE PERIOD WHERE I'M MOST LIKELY TO NOD OFF.

TRIG HAS THE MOST PILLOWESQUE TEXTBOOK.

NO FAIR. IN GEOMETRY WE GOT THESE BRICK THINGS.

NICOLE, LOOK! BOBBY WHITMEYER MUST'VE TRANSFERRED INTO OUR HISTORY CLASS!

HE'S THE HUNKIEST HUNK IN THE SCHOOL! HE IS SOOO HOT! SOOO BABE-LIKE! SOOO TO DIE FOR!

...SOOO STUPID...

OH, LIKE BRAINS REALLY MATTER.

OOPS— I'M IN THE WRONG ROOM.

IN THIS CASE THEY DO.

AAAA! COME BACK!

ROGER'S AT THE OFFICE... THE KIDS ARE BACK AT SCHOOL...

FINALLY, I HAVE SOME PEACE AND QUIET. FINALLY, I HAVE THE HOUSE TO MYSELF.

NO MORE WAITING FOR THE KIDS TO FINISH THEIR GAMES. TODAY, I'VE GOT A CHANCE TO REALLY GET SOMETHING DONE.

BING!

LET'S SEE... NOW I'VE BEEN TO MYST ISLAND AND THE MECHANICAL AGE...

Splish Splash Clunk... Splish Splash Clunk...

FoxTrot
BILL AMEND

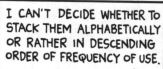

I CAN FIGURE OUT MULTI-VARIABLE CALCULUS EQUATIONS.

I CAN FIGURE OUT THE CUBE ROOT OF ANY 20-DIGIT NUMBER.

I CAN FIGURE OUT SINES AND COSINES WITHOUT CONSULTING A TABLE.

BUT, MAN, I CAN'T FIGURE **YOU** OUT.

LOOK, I HAPPEN TO THINK "FULL HOUSE" IS FUNNY, OK?!

DADDY, YOU HAVE TO GO TALK TO JASON!

OH?

HE RENTED THIS NEW "PRIMAL INSTINCT" VIDEO GAME WHERE YOU FIGHT THESE MONSTERS AND SCORE POINTS BY RIPPING THEIR HEADS OFF! YOU SEE THE VEINS DANGLING AND EVERYTHING! IT'S TOTALLY DISGUSTING AND VIOLENT!

HE'S BEEN PLAYING IT WITH MARCUS ALL EVENING!

SO YOU WANT ME TO TELL HIM HE'S TOO YOUNG FOR THIS SORT OF THING?

NO, I WANT YOU TO TELL HIM TO LET ME PLAY, TOO!

WHY DO THESE SITUATIONS ALWAYS SEEM TO DEVELOP ON NIGHTS WHEN I'M IN CHARGE?

JASON, YOUR STUPID IGUANA IS LOOSE AGAIN!

HE'S HERE IN THE FAMILY ROOM CHEWING THROUGH THE CABLES TO YOUR NINTENDO MACHINE!

CAN'T SAY I DIDN'T TRY TO TELL YOU!

UM, JASON'S NOT HOME.

I KNOW.

FoxTrot
BILL AMEND

AAAA! I'M DEAD!

PAIGE, WHAT'S WRONG?

I HAVE TO GIVE A THREE-MINUTE SPEECH FOR MY SOCIAL STUDIES CLASS ON FRIDAY! THAT'S ONLY A FEW DAYS AWAY!

WHAT WILL I DO?! I'M DEAD! THERE'S JUST NOT ENOUGH TIME TO PREPARE!

I'M SURE YOU'LL THINK OF SOMETHING TO SAY.

SAY SCHMAY! I'LL NEED TO GET MY CUTE NEW SKIRT DRY CLEANED!

YOU KNOW, PAIGE, THE PHRASE "STYLE OVER SUBSTANCE" WASN'T MEANT TO BE A CREDO.

NICOLE, I CAN'T BELIEVE I HAVE TO GIVE A THREE-MINUTE SPEECH FOR SOCIAL STUDIES CLASS!

MY TEACHER'S GONE INSANE! WHAT IS SHE THINKING?!

HOW CAN I POSSIBLY TALK ABOUT ANYTHING FOR THREE MINUTES STRAIGHT?!

...SAYS THE GIRL WHO'S BEEN ON THE PHONE FOR TWO HOURS.

AND LET ME TELL YOU HOW SYMPATHETIC MY MOTHER IS BEING...

WHAT ARE YOU WATCHING?

C-SPAN.

I HAVE TO GIVE A SPEECH IN MY SOCIAL STUDIES CLASS ON FRIDAY.

I THOUGHT WATCHING ALL THESE POLITICIANS GIVING TALKS IN NEW HAMPSHIRE MIGHT GIVE ME SOME POINTERS.

GOING THE BROWN-NOSE ROUTE, I TAKE IT.

WELL, I DON'T HAVE TIME TO REALLY PREPARE ANYTHING TOO INSIGHTFUL.

HEH HEH HEH...

HEE HEE HEE...

WAA HA HA HA HA (COUGH) HA HA HA!

AMEND

(SNIFF) OH, MAN...

WHY THE ANGRY FACE? I THINK YOUR SPEECH'S OPENING JOKE IS REALLY FUNNY.

THERE IS NO OPENING JOKE!

OK, PAIGE, IT'S JUST A THREE-MINUTE SPEECH. DON'T BE NERVOUS.

DO WHAT DAD SAID: IMAGINE EVERYONE IS IN THEIR UNDERWEAR.

YOWZA! IT'S LIKE A CHIPPENDALES SHOW!

I'VE REALLY GOT TO STOP LISTENING TO DAD.

MISS FOX, CAN WE GET THIS STARTED SOMETIME TODAY?

AMEND

I SURVIVED MY SPEECH! I SURVIVED MY SPEECH!

I DIDN'T FAINT... I DIDN'T THROW UP... I ONLY GARBLED THREE OR FOUR WORDS...

MY SPEECH IS OVER! WEEEEEEEEE!

MISS FOX, IT'S CUSTOMARY TO DO THAT AWAY FROM THE PODIUM.

HEH HEH... SORRY.

AMEND

FoxTrot
BILL AMEND

41

MOM, DAD, WOULD IT BE OK FOR ME TO GET AN ADVANCE ON MY ALLOWANCE?

WHAT FOR?

DENISE AND I STARTED DATING EXACTLY ONE YEAR AGO THIS WEEK AND I WANTED TO GET HER AN ANNIVERSARY GIFT.

PETER, THAT'S SO SWEET... SO THOUGHTFUL. SO ROMANTIC.

THANKS.

OBVIOUSLY MY GENES AT WORK.

SHEESH. FORGET A WOMAN'S BIRTHDAY FOUR OR FIVE TIMES AND YOU HEAR ABOUT IT FOREVER.

PAIGE, HELP ME OUT. I CAN'T DECIDE WHAT TO GET DENISE FOR OUR ANNIVERSARY.

LET'S SEE... YOU'VE BEEN DATING FOR ONE YEAR, RIGHT?

RIGHT.

THAT'S 52 WEEKS WITH YOU AS HER BOYFRIEND... 52 WEEKS WITH YOU AS A PIVOTAL PLAYER IN HER LIFE... 52 WEEKS WITH YOU AS THE CENTER OF HER EMOTIONAL UNIVERSE.

ANY SUGGESTIONS?

DOES MAALOX COME GIFT-WRAPPED?

WHAT SHOULD I GET DENISE?... WHAT SHOULD I GET DENISE?...

I COULD GET HER THAT CHOCOLATE-SCENTED PERFUME. DENISE LOVES CHOCOLATE.

THERE'S NO CHOCOLATE-SCENTED PERFUME, YOU FOOL.

SURE THERE IS. THEY HAVE TV COMMERCIALS FOR IT ALL THE TIME. SHOOT — WHAT'S IT CALLED?...

COCO. BY CHANEL.

PETER, GIVE ME THE MONEY AND LET ME GO BUY THE GIFT.

WHO AM I KIDDING? I CAN'T AFFORD TO GET DENISE ANYTHING NICE FOR OUR ANNIVERSARY.

PERFUME'S TOO EXPENSIVE... JEWELRY'S TOO EXPENSIVE... ISOTONER GLOVES ARE TOO EXPENSIVE...

YOU KNOW, SON, THERE **IS** SOMETHING EXTRA SPECIAL YOU CAN GIVE HER THAT WON'T COST YOU **ANY** MONEY.

DAD, I ALREADY TOLD YOU, I DON'T WANT YOUR OPERA TICKETS!

PLEEE-EASE??

ROGER, THOSE ARE OURS!

HAPPY ANNIVERSARY, DENISE.

HAPPY ANNIVERSARY, PETER.

I, UM, WANTED TO GET YOU SOMETHING REALLY SPECIAL, BUT I COULDN'T AFFORD ANYTHING I LIKED.

THAT'S OK. TAKING THIS WALK WITH ME IS SPECIAL.

STILL, I **DO** HAVE A LITTLE GIFT FOR YOU...

WHAT ARE YOU DOING?

TA DA

DID YOU TAPE WRAPPING PAPER TO YOUR **LIPS**?

363... 364... 365.

WHAT A WONDERFUL ANNIVERSARY GIFT, PETER — A KISS FOR EVERY DAY WE'VE BEEN TOGETHER.

GLAD YOU LIKED IT.

NOT THAT "HOURS" OR "MINUTES" WOULDN'T HAVE BEEN BETTER.

YOU KNOW, MAYBE THIS WAS A LEAP YEAR...

FoxTrot
BILL AMEND

Name: Peter Fox

Date: Not as often as I'd like to, sadly.

1. A projectile is fired from a cannon at a 30-degree angle with the ground and an initial velocity of 100 m/sec. Assuming no air resistance and $g = 10$ m/sec^2, calculate the time it will spend in the air.

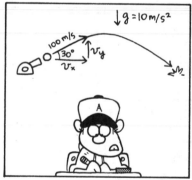

TIME'S UP, EVERYONE. PLEASE PASS YOUR TESTS FORWARD.

DOODLERS SHOULD **NOT** TAKE PHYSICS.

SHOOTING FOR AN "A" FOR "APPALLING," ARE WE, MR. FOX?

HOW WAS SCHOOL?

GREAT! WE'RE HAVING OUR FIRST MATH TEST ON WEDNESDAY!

MISS O'MALLEY SAID IT'S GOING TO BE REALLY HARD, TOO. IT'LL COVER THE FIRST THREE CHAPTERS IN OUR TEXTBOOK.

Elementary Mathematics

SHE SAID IF PEOPLE DON'T STUDY FOR IT, THEY MAY HAVE REAL PROBLEMS GETTING A PASSING GRADE.

WELL, THEN, YOU'D BETTER GET CRACKING.

MOTHER, PLEASE. SHE WAS SPEAKING TO THE MORTALS.

AMEND

MOM SUGGESTED I STUDY SOME FOR TOMORROW'S BIG MATH TEST.

IMAGINE... ME, JASON FOX, KING OF MATHEMATICS, STUDYING FOR A MEASLY TEST ABOUT FRACTIONS AND DECIMALS!

Kids! Visit the Sludge Man Web Site!!!   SLUDGE MAN

HA!

AMEND

MOMS CAN BE SO FOOLISH SOMETIMES.

YOU LOOK CHIPPER.

YOU BET. TODAY'S MY MATH TEST.

THE ONE YOU DIDN'T STUDY FOR.

MOM, I KEEP TELLING YOU, I DON'T NEED TO STUDY.

AMEND

WHEN IT COMES TO MATH, I'M LIKE A HUMAN SUPER-COMPUTER! THIS STUFF IS IN MY BLOOD! I CAN DO IT ALL ON INSTINCT! NO SWEAT!

...USUALLY.

JASON, I SAID TIME'S UP.

OK, EVERYONE, I'VE HAD A CHANCE TO GRADE YOUR MATH TESTS.

VERY GOOD, JASON. YOU GOT A 102. THAT'S AN A+.

OH YESSSSSSS...

VERY, **VERY** GOOD, EILEEN. YOU GOT A 104.

OH **NO!**

ISN'T IT GREAT, JASON?? YOU AND I EACH GOT AN A+ ON OUR MATH TEST!

YOU GOT 102 PERCENT AND I GOT 104 PERCENT! I'VE NEVER GOTTEN AN A+ BEFORE!

I'M ACTUALLY KINDA SURPRISED YOU DIDN'T GET ALL OF THE EXTRA-CREDIT PROBLEM RIGHT. I THOUGHT IT WAS PRETTY EASY AND YOU **NORMALLY** GET THE BEST GRADE IN THE CLASS.

YOU KNOW, FOR SOMEONE WHO JUST GOT AN A+, YOU DON'T LOOK TOO HAPPY.

WILL YOU JUST LET ME WRITHE IN PEACE?!

SWEETIE, WHAT'S WRONG?

STUPID EILEEN JACOBSON GOT A BETTER SCORE THAN ME ON THE MATH TEST!

THAT'S WHAT HAPPENS WHEN YOU DON'T STUDY.

MOTHER, THE KING OF MATH HAS BEEN DETHRONED BY A GIRL!... DID YOU HEAR ME? A **GIRL!!!**

THE LOWEST OF THE LOW! THE VILEST OF THE VILE! THE SLIMIEST OF ALL CREATURES! AND NOW ONE OF THEIR WRETCHED ILK HAS BEATEN ME AT MATH! IT'S MORE THAN I CAN STAND!

SPEAKING AS ONE OF THE WRETCHED: "BUMMER."

I'M NOT SENSING THE KIND OF SYMPATHY I THINK I DESERVE. WHERE'S DAD?

I STILL CAN'T BELIEVE I GOT THE HIGHEST GRADE ON THE MATH TEST! IT'S LIKE A DREAM COME TRUE!

LOOK, EILEEN, THE ONLY REASON YOU GOT A HIGHER GRADE THAN ME IS BECAUSE I **LET** YOU GET A HIGHER GRADE THAN ME! OK?!

♡ REALLY? ♡ THAT'S SO ♡ SWEET. ♡

NO! NO! THAT'S NOT WHAT I MEANT! AAAAA!

AAAA! AS IF IT WEREN'T BAD ENOUGH THAT EILEEN JACOBSON BEAT ME ON THE MATH TEST!...

... NOW SHE'S **LOOKING** AT ME ALL STRANGE!

HOW SO?

SAY "150-MEGAHERTZ POWERPC PROCESSOR."

150-MEGAHERTZ POWERPC PROCESSOR.

♡ LIKE ♡ THIS. ♡

YOU KNOW, I SHOULD THINK **MOST** PEOPLE WOULD LOOK AT YOU STRANGELY.

WHAT DID YOU MEAN WHEN YOU SAID YOU **LET** ME GET THE HIGHEST GRADE ON THE MATH TEST?

WELL, THE TRUTH IS I DIDN'T REALLY STUDY FOR IT.

THAT'S WHY I GOOFED UP THE EXTRA-CREDIT PROBLEM. **HAD** I STUDIED, I DEFINITELY WOULD HAVE GOTTEN A PERFECT 106 PERCENT, WHICH WOULD HAVE BEATEN YOUR SCORE OF 104. INSTEAD, I GOT A LOUSY 102.

LET ME GET THIS STRAIGHT: I STUDIED AND GOT MY BEST GRADE EVER; YOU **DIDN'T** STUDY AND GOT A GRADE YOU DON'T LIKE.

RIGHT. SO THAT MEANS I'M SMARTER.

UM, IF YOU SAY SO.

HECK, NAME ONE THING I STILL NEED TO LEARN!

MY PARENTS WERE SO EXCITED THAT I GOT THE HIGH GRADE ON THE MATH TEST THAT THEY WANT TO TAKE ME OUT FOR ICE CREAM.

I THOUGHT MAYBE YOU'D LIKE TO COME, TOO. THEY'D PAY, OF COURSE.

BOY, THAT'S A NO-BRAINER.

OH, GOOD. WE'LL PICK YOU UP AT 7:30.

WAIT! NO! YOU MISUNDERSTOOD!...

SO DO YOU WANT TO GO OUT FOR ICE CREAM WITH MY FAMILY AND ME?

WELL, I WOULD NEED MY PARENTS' PERMISSION.

AND TO BE HONEST, I REALLY DON'T SEE THEM GIVING IT TO ME.

OH.

SEEING AS I'D RATHER DIE THAN ASK.

MAYBE I SHOULD HAVE MY MOM CALL YOUR MOM...

JASON'S GOT A DA-ATE! JASON'S GOT A DA-ATE!

IT'S NOT A DATE! HER PARENTS ARE TAKING US OUT FOR ICE CREAM!

JASON'S GOT A GIRLL-FRIEND! JASON'S GOT A GIRLL-FRIEND!

SHE'S NOT MY GIRL-FRIEND! I DON'T EVEN LIKE GIRLS!

JASON'S IN LOO-OOVE! JASON'S IN LOO-OOVE!

THIS WAS HER IDEA, NOT MINE! I'M JUST GOING FOR THE FREE CHOCOLATE SUNDAE!

IT'S GOT TO BE TOUGH TEASING SOMEONE WHEN YOU'RE REALLY, REALLY JEALOUS.

OH, SHUT UP.

JASON, I THINK EILEEN AND HER PARENTS JUST PULLED INTO THE DRIVEWAY.

WOULD YOU MIND IF I INVITED THEM IN? WE'RE ALL SIMPLY DYING TO MEET THIS GIRL.

OH, WAIT— THEY JUST PULLED OUT. IT MUST NOT BE THEM. NEVER MIND.

I'M NOT GOING TO ASK WHY YOU WERE WAITING FOR US OUT IN YOUR BUSHES. ON THE WAY BACK, DO YOU THINK YOU COULD DROP ME OFF A BLOCK OR TWO AWAY?

I THINK YOU SHOULD ORDER THE KING KONG SUNDAE. ARE YOU INSANE?! THAT'S LIKE A MILLION SCOOPS OF ICE CREAM!

C'MON, YOU'RE A GUY — YOU CAN EAT IT.

PLEASE?? DO IT FOR ME?? PLEASE??

THIS IS NOT A GOOD SIGN, OLD BOY. I CAN'T BELIEVE YOU REALLY ORDERED ONE OF THOSE!

LET'S SIT IN THIS LITTLE BOOTH OVER HERE. BUT THERE'S A BIGGER BOOTH OVER THERE.

... AND ANOTHER OVER THERE.

WHY WOULD YOU WANT TO SIT IN THE SMALLEST BOOTH THEY'VE GOT?!

OOPS—SORRY. IS THAT YOUR FOOT I KEEP BUMPING? YOU NEVER ANSWERED MY QUESTION.

FoxTrot
BILL AMEND

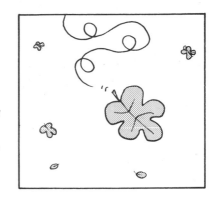

FoxTrot
BILL AMEND

AWOOOO!

TRY HOWLING A LITTLE BIT HIGHER.

I COULD STAND ON THAT CHAIR OVER THERE...

THAT'S NOT WHAT I MEANT.

UM, MOM, YOU PROBABLY DON'T WANT TO GO DOWN INTO THE BASEMENT ANYTIME SOON.

WHY'S THAT?

JASON AND MARCUS HAVE BEEN DECORATING IT FOR HALLOWEEN.

AND YOU THINK THEY'VE MADE IT TOO SCARY FOR ME?

NOT EXACTLY.

YOU THINK THEY'VE MADE IT TOO GORY FOR ME?

NOT THAT, EITHER.

WHAT, THEN?

LET'S JUST SAY IT **WOULD** MAKE YOU SCREAM.

I **TOLD** YOU NOT TO STAPLE-GUN THOSE BATS TO THE WATER HEATER.

WHAT ARE YOU DOING?

WE HAVE TO WRITE A GHOST STORY FOR ENGLISH CLASS.

MY TEACHER SAID THE SCARIER WE MAKE IT, THE BETTER THE GRADE WE'LL GET.

SOUNDS LIKE A FUN ASSIGNMENT.

I'M CERTAINLY ENJOYING IT.

"What's to be afraid of?" thought Jason as he entered the creaky old house just before midnight...

"All I see are cobwebs," thought Jason as he surveyed the old house.

"No ghosts here," he chuckled to himself.

He was, of course, about to be proven wrong.

...BIG TIME.

SINCE WHEN DO YOU GIGGLE DOING HOMEWORK?

As the clock struck 12:00, Jason had a chilling realization.

"How could that clock still be working?" he asked himself. "This house has been boarded up for 20 years!"

Suddenly, the clock became the least of his worries.

PETER, IF YOU SAW AN AX-WIELDING GHOST, WOULD YOU SAY "AAAA!" OR "AIEEE!"?

HOW COME I NEVER GET HOMEWORK ASSIGNMENTS LIKE THIS?

As Jason ran to escape the ax-wielding ghost, the floorboards suddenly gave way.

Down, Jason fell, into the dark and murky basement.

"I wonder why the ghost didn't follow me down here," he mused.

"Because it's already too crowded," came the reply from all directions.

"aaaa!" screamed Jason, as the ghosts raised their axes.

Suddenly, he was at home. In his bed. It had all been just a bad dream.

Or had it?

I JUST LOVE HAPPY ENDINGS.

I THOUGHT YOU WERE WRITING A GHOST STORY.

HOW DID YOUR ENGLISH TEACHER LIKE YOUR GHOST STORY?

WELL, YOU KNOW HOW I TRIED REALLY HARD TO MAKE IT GOOD AND GORY?

WHICH YOU DEFINITELY DID.

YES, WELL, I THINK I MAY HAVE DONE TOO GOOD A JOB.

HOW SO?

HE GAVE ME AN "A" PLUS...

HECK, WHAT'S WRONG WITH THAT?

I MEAN, HE GAVE ME AN "A," PLUS AN APPOINTMENT WITH THE SCHOOL COUNSELOR.

RELAX. I GET THAT ALL THE TIME.

FoxTrot
BILL AMEND

WHAT ARE YOU DOING?

FLIP FLIP
FLIP FLIP FLIP
FLIP

I HAVE TO SOME-HOW WRITE A BOOK REPORT ON "MOBY DICK" IN THE NEXT HOUR AND A HALF BEFORE SCHOOL.

AND, OF COURSE, YOU HAVEN'T READ ANY OF IT.

I FIGURE MY ONLY HOPE AT THIS POINT IS TO FAN THROUGH THE PAGES AND PRAY THAT MY SUBCONSCIOUS MIND WILL ABSORB ALL THE TEXT.

I TRIED SOMETHING LIKE THAT BEFORE MY FRENCH VOCABULARY TEST.

DID IT WORK?

OUI. I MEAN, NON.

Moby Dick, by Herman Melville, is a classic American novel.

About a whale. And some sailors.

In conclusion,...

YOU KNOW, SOME MIGHT ARGUE THAT IT'S A STROKE OF IRONIC GENIUS TO REDUCE A 432-PAGE BOOK DOWN TO SIX CHOICE SENTENCES!

PETER, YOUR NAME AND THE DATE DOESN'T COUNT AS A SENTENCE.

DID YOU HEAR ABOUT OUR SON PETER'S LITTLE ADVENTURE THIS MORNING?

HE TRIED TO READ "MOBY DICK" AND WRITE A REPORT ABOUT IT IN THE TIME BETWEEN BREAKFAST AND SCHOOL. HIS PROCRAS-TINATION HAS GOTTEN TOTALLY OUT OF HAND.

NORMALLY, I'D WANT YOU TO GO UP AND HAVE A LITTLE TALK WITH HIM, BUT IN THIS CASE...

... I WISH YOU'D STOP HAVING LITTLE TALKS WITH HIM!

HEE HEE... DID I EVER TELL YOU HOW I WROTE MY ENTIRE SENIOR THESIS IN ONE NIGHT?

FoxTrot
BILL AMEND

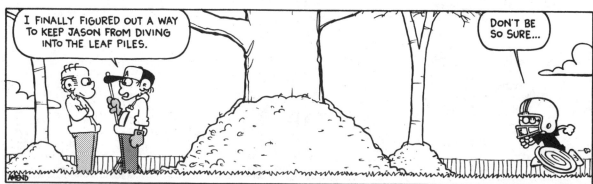

59

...SO THEN I TOLD HIM GLOG BLURDTH UXH N INTO THE GLUFTH SOQ...

...WHICH **HE** TOOK TO MEAN FUB THE COMPUTER NOMF SHUMX BLOO GOOLTH!

YOU NEVER LAUGH AT MY STORIES.

NOT THAT **YOU** AREN'T LAUGHABLE ON OCCASION.

THAT'S NOT DINNER YOU'RE COOKING, IS IT?

YUP. BRUSSELS SPROUT STEW.

WITH TOASTED EGGPLANT CHIPS.

AND WARM GINGER PUDDING FOR DESSERT.

ARE YOU SURE IT'S SAFE TO SHUT OFF POWER TO THE KITCHEN?

SAFER THAN THE ALTERNATIVE.

WHICH SWEATER DO YOU LIKE BETTER, DADDY? THIS BLUE ONE...

THIS BROWN ONE...

OR THIS GREEN ONE?

I LIKE WHICHEVER ONE IS THE CHEAPEST.

YOU KNOW, APART FROM PAYING FOR ALL THIS, YOU'RE NO HELP WHATSOEVER.

THOSE ONES MARKED "90 PERCENT OFF" ARE CUTE...

60

FoxTrot
BILL AMEND

FoxTrot

BILL AMEND

LOOK, NICOLE! HE WROTE ME ANOTHER NOTE!

NO WAY! WHAT'S IT SAY?!

Dear Paige,
I think you are the hottest girl in the entire school.
Love,
Your secret admirer

OBVIOUSLY, I DON'T KNOW ANYTHING ABOUT THIS GUY...

...BUT I CAN TELL HE IS **VERY** PERCEPTIVE.

NONSENSE. HE'S OBVIOUSLY SOMEHOW OVERLOOKED **ME**.

MOM, DID YOU EVER GET NOTES FROM A SECRET ADMIRER WHEN YOU WERE IN SCHOOL?

NOT IN SCHOOL, BUT THE YEAR AFTER COLLEGE I DID.

I WAS LIVING IN AN APARTMENT AND SOMEONE KEPT SLIPPING ANONYMOUS LOVE LETTERS UNDER MY DOOR.

DID YOU EVER MEET HIM?! WHAT WAS HE LIKE?!

WELL, HE TURNED OUT TO BE A REAL NERD. NOT AT ALL WHAT I EXPECTED.

OH.

...BUT I MARRIED HIM ANYWAY.

I HEARD THAT.

THIS SECRET ADMIRER OF MINE MUST REALLY, REALLY LIKE ME.

HIS FIRST NOTE SAID I WAS TOTALLY CUTE, HIS NEXT ONE SAID I WAS TOTALLY HOT AND TODAY'S NOTE SAYS I'M TOTALLY PERFECT.

I WONDER WHAT HIS **NEXT** NOTE WILL SAY...

HOW ABOUT "TOTALLY GODDESS-LIKE"?

I CAN'T BELIEVE MY STUPID SISTER IS FALLING FOR THESE.

PAIGE, SWEETIE, I KNOW YOU'RE HURTING.

I KNOW YOU'D PROBABLY LIKE NOTHING BETTER RIGHT NOW THAN TO PUNCH YOUR BROTHER PETER'S LIGHTS OUT.

BUT IF YOU COULD JUST PUT ASIDE THAT ANGER FOR A SECOND...

PAIGE? UM, I'M REALLY, REALLY SORRY.

PETER, IS THAT CATCHER'S MASK REALLY NECESSARY?

I CAN'T HEAR YOU, PETER. STEP A LITTLE CLOSER...

PAIGE, GEEZ— I SAID I WAS SORRY.

PETER, WHAT YOU DID TO ME TODAY WAS AS MEAN AS ANYTHING YOU'VE EVER DONE.

THIS PAST WEEK, WHEN I READ THOSE NOTES, FOR THE FIRST TIME IN MY LIFE I FELT REALLY ATTRACTIVE AND SPECIAL. I FELT LIKE SOMEONE OUT THERE REALLY CARED ABOUT ME. AND TODAY WAS THE DAY I WAS GOING TO MEET HIM. DO YOU HAVE ANY IDEA HOW HAPPY AND NERVOUS AND EXCITED I WAS?!

THEN **YOU** POP OUT AND LAUGH, "HA HA HA, SUCKER— IT WAS ALL JUST A JOKE!" WELL, IT WASN'T A JOKE TO ME AND IT CERTAINLY WASN'T WHAT I WOULD CALL **FUNNY!**

BUT HOW WAS **I** SUPPOSED TO KNOW THAT?

PETER, YOU **ARE** SORRY.

PAIGE IS PRETTY MAD AT YOU, HUH?

YEAH.

I PULLED A PRETTY THOUGHTLESS PRANK ON HER AT SCHOOL. I DIDN'T REALIZE SHE WOULD TAKE IT SO HARD.

SHE SAYS THERE'S NOTHING I CAN DO TO MAKE UP FOR WHAT I DID.

UM, SINCE WHEN DO **YOU** BAKE COOKIES?

SHE DID SAY THERE ARE WAYS I CAN **BEGIN** TO MAKE UP...

FoxTrot
BILL AMEND

WHO WANTS TO GO CHRISTMAS SHOPPING WITH ME? PETER??

PAIGE, GET A LIFE! IT'S NOT EVEN DECEMBER!

SO WHAT? **TELL** ME YOU'RE NOT DYING TO HIT THE MALLS! **TELL** ME YOU DON'T LIE AWAKE AT NIGHT PLANNING WHAT STORES YOU'LL GO TO FIRST! **TELL** ME YOU DON'T CHOKE ON YOUR DROOL EVERY TIME YOU HEAR THE WORD "NORDSTROM"!

DON'T LIE— I CAN SEE IT IN YOUR EYES.

OH, WAIT— THAT'S MY REFLECTION.

PAIGE, I'M GOING TO COUNT TO 10, AS QUICKLY AS I CAN...

HOW'S YOUR NEW VIDEO GAME?

GREAT, I THINK. I HAVEN'T REALLY PLAYED IT YET.

THEN WHAT ARE YOU DOING?

THESE GAMES ALWAYS HAVE SECRET CHEAT CODES THAT MAKE YOU INVINCIBLE AND STUFF, SO I'M METHODICALLY TRYING EVERY BUTTON COMBINATION, HOPING TO FIND ONE. ONCE I DO, I CAN GO ON THE INTERNET AND TRADE FOR ALL THE REST.

I SHOULD BE READY TO PLAY THIS NEXT TUESDAY OR WEDNESDAY.

I SEE A LOT OF BOARD GAMES COMING YOUR WAY THIS CHRISTMAS.

I MEAN, WHAT'S THE POINT OF PLAYING IF YOU CAN'T WIN EVERY TIME?

"...NEVER SEND TO KNOW FOR WHOM THE BELCH TOLLS; IT TOLLS FOR THEE."

"BELL," YOU MORON.

IT'S "FOR WHOM THE **BELL** TOLLS"!

BRAAAP!

I BELIEVE YOU STAND CORRECTED.

YOU KNOW, MY FRIENDS AT SCHOOL THINK I MAKE THESE STORIES UP.

Mary Beth has baked an apple pie.

Her father wants a piece twice as big as her mother's piece. Her brother wants a piece twice as big as Mary Beth's piece. Mary Beth wants a piece 2/3 as big as her father's piece.

If she divides the pie so that no extra pieces remain, what fraction of the pie goes to her brother?

First of all, why she would even give any pie to her brother...

BAD NEWS, PAIGE. QUINCY THREW UP ON YOUR TOOTHBRUSH.

THIS WORLD WIDE WEB IS PRETTY COOL. I MEAN, IF I WANTED TO, I COULD ACCESS NASA PHOTOS...

I COULD GO INTO THE LIBRARY OF CONGRESS AND READ HISTORICAL TEXTS...

I COULD STUDY THE ART COLLECTIONS OF NUMEROUS EUROPEAN MUSEUMS...

EMPHASIS ON "IF YOU WANTED TO."

OOO – MISS DECEMBER LIKES ICE CREAM! ME, TOO!

NUCLEAR MISSILES CAN'T DESTROY PLASMA-MAN.

LASERS ONLY MAKE HIM STRONGER.

HE'S IMPERVIOUS TO EVERY WEAPON TECHNOLOGY KNOWN TO MAN.

BUT SPILL ONE LOUSY GLASS OF GRAPE JUICE...

HERE'S A SPONGE. IS IT RUINED?

FoxTrot
BILL AMEND

FoxTrot
BILL AMEND

TYPETY TYPE TYPETY TYPE
TYPETY TYPETY TYPETY
TYPE TYPETY TYPE TYPE
TYPETY TYPE TYPETY TYPE

WHAM!

MAIL

SANTA'S REALLY GOT TO GET AN INTERNET ADDRESS.

JUST HOW MANY BOXES DID YOUR CHRISTMAS LIST **FILL**?!

NEIMAN MARCUS?! YOU WENT SHOPPING AT NEIMAN MARCUS?!

HUH?

ISN'T THEIR STUFF GREAT?! ISN'T THEIR STUFF AMAZING?! WHADJA GET?! LEMME SEE! LEMME SEE!

TWO QUESTIONS: DID YOU GET THAT DEAD RAT OUT OF THE BASEMENT, AND WHAT ON EARTH HAS GOTTEN INTO YOUR SISTER?!

MOM, NEXT TIME I ASK FOR A PAPER BAG...

HEY, JASON — UP FOR A GAME OF CHESS?

SURE. CAN I BE WHITE?

OK.

E2 - E4
F1 - C4
D1 - F3
F3 × F7
CHECKMATE. I WIN.

THANKS, DAD, THAT WAS FUN.

METHINKS MY GAME MAY BE GETTING A BIT TOO PREDICTABLE.

PAIGE, YOUR MOTHER ASKED ME TO MAKE YOU KIDS' LUNCHES TODAY. WHAT KIND OF SANDWICH DO YOU LIKE?

OH, I DON'T CARE. PEANUT BUTTER AND JELLY... BOLOGNA AND CHEESE... TUNA FISH... WHATEVER.

GOTCHA.

MY FATHER IS NOT OF THIS EARTH.

A PEANUT BUTTER, TUNA FISH, BOLOGNA, JELLY AND CHEESE SANDWICH?!

FoxTrot
BILL AMEND

FoxTrot
BILL AMEND

A BLANKET OF SNOW OUTDOORS...

A CRACKLING FIRE IN THE FIREPLACE...

A BIG MUG OF HOT COCOA...

JOHNNY MATHIS ON THE STEREO...

YOU KNOW, ROGER, THIS REALLY MAY BE ONE OF OUR NICEST CHRISTMAS EVES EVER.

THEY WERE OUT OF "IT'S A WONDERFUL LIFE," SO WE RENTED "TERMINATOR 2."

...WIDE-SCREEN EDITION.

GIVEN OUR TRACK RECORD, THAT MAY NOT BE TOO DIFFICULT.

SPEAKING OF WHICH, I'D BETTER CHECK ON PAIGE'S COOKIES.

I COULDN'T FIND THE BAKING SODA, SO I USED DIET PEPSI. IS THAT OK?

AAAA! DOOMATHON II! I GOT DOOMATHON II!

IT'S SUPPOSED TO BE THE BEST COMPUTER GAME EVER! EXPLODING BULLETS... SLO-MO DECAPITATIONS... 16-BIT STEREO GUT-SPLATTER SOUND EFFECTS... OVER 10 TIMES THE KILLING ACTION OF DOOMATHON I...

OH, THANK YOU, SANTA! THANK YOU! THANK YOU!

I MUST'VE BEEN EXTRA NICE THIS YEAR.

JASON, I DON'T LIKE YOU PLAYING THIS COMPUTER GAME. IT'S TOO VIOLENT. BUT SANTA GAVE IT TO ME!

SANTA MADE A MISTAKE. BUT LOOK AT HOW MUCH FUN IT IS!...

Blam! Blam! Blam! Blam! Blam! Blam! Blam!

GOSH, ALL THE THRILLS OF A BUTCHER SHOP. WAIT—IT'LL GET BETTER ONCE I FIND THE BAZOOKA.

I'M TELLING YOU, MOM, YOU'LL CHANGE YOUR OPINION OF DOOMATHON II ONCE YOU'VE PLAYED IT. JASON, I REALLY DON'T THINK SO.

LOOK OUT! THERE'S A CYBER-GHOUL! SHOOT HIM! Blam! Blam! Blam! Blam! Blam! Blam! Blam! Blam! Splat!

WAY TO GO, MOM! YOU BLEW HIS HEAD OFF! I DON'T MIND TELLING YOU, JASON, THIS IS VERY, VERY DISTURBING.

BECAUSE IT'S SO GORY? BECAUSE I WANT TO KEEP PLAYING. OOO—I FOUND A BIGGER SHOTGUN.

MOM, CAN I USE THE COMPUTER AT SOME POINT? IT IS, AFTER ALL, MY GAME.

JUST LET ME PLAY A FEW MORE MINUTES...

Blam! Blam! Blam! Blam! Blam! Blam! Blam! Blam! Blam! Blam! Blam!

Blam! Blam! Blam! Blam! Blam! Blam! Blam! Blam! Blam! Blam! Blam!

MOM, C'MON, THAT'S WHAT YOU SAID LAST NIGHT.

YOU MISSED A GREAT SUNRISE, BY THE WAY.

ANDY, **LOOK** AT YOU! YOU'VE BEEN PLAYING THAT DOOMATHON GAME ALL WEEK!

YOU DON'T EAT... YOU DON'T SLEEP... FOR YEARS YOU'VE RAILED AGAINST VIOLENCE IN VIDEO GAMES AND HERE YOU ARE, GLUED TO THE WORST OF THE LOT!

WHAT DO YOU HAVE TO SAY FOR YOURSELF?!

I NEED MORE COFFEE— MY TRIGGER FINGER IS SLOWING DOWN.

YOU KNOW, YOU WEREN'T THIS SYMPATHETIC WHEN I WENT ON MY TWISTER BINGE.

WHERE HAVE **YOU** BEEN?

AT THE COMPUTER STORE. I TRADED IN MY DOOMATHON II GAME FOR SIM-MOONWALK.

HOW COME?

MOM CONVINCED ME THAT I WAS TOO YOUNG TO HAVE A GAME LIKE THAT IN THE HOUSE.

BUT I THOUGHT SHE **LIKED** IT— SHE'S BEEN PLAYING IT NIGHT AND DAY.

THAT'S WHAT CONVINCED ME. I MEAN, **I** CAN'T DO MY LAUNDRY.

I GUESS THIS MEANS NO MORE FROOT LOOPS FOR DINNER.

NOW I'LL NEVER KNOW THE SECRET TO LEVEL 83!

FoxTrot
BILL AMEND

WHAT'S WITH YOU?

THIS NEW YEAR IS OFF TO ONE MISERABLE START.

SOMEONE ATE ALL THE CHOCO HONEY FLAKES, I SQUIRTED MY EYE WITH THIS STUPID GRAPEFRUIT, AND TO TOP IT ALL OFF, THERE'S NO "CALVIN" IN THE COMICS!

LOOK ON THE BRIGHT SIDE, PAIGE — THINGS COULD BE WAY WORSE.

OH, YEAH? HOW?

HEH HEH, HAVE YOU BEEN IN YOUR CLOSET LATELY?

JASON, IF THAT IGUANA CHEWED UP ANY MORE OF MY SHOES...

AMEND

MOM, I'M AFRAID TO ASK, BUT WHAT'S FOR DINNER?

I THOUGHT I'D MAKE A PIZZA.

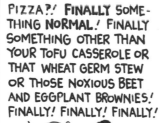
PIZZA?! **FINALLY** SOMETHING **NORMAL**! FINALLY SOMETHING OTHER THAN YOUR TOFU CASSEROLE OR THAT WHEAT GERM STEW OR THOSE NOXIOUS BEET AND EGGPLANT BROWNIES! FINALLY! FINALLY! FINALLY!

AND I'M REALLY HUNGRY, TOO.

UM, WHAT'S WITH THE CARTON OF LIMA BEANS?

YOU DIDN'T ASK WHAT SORT OF PIZZA...

AMEND

WHAT ARE YOU DOING?

I'M WRITING A COMPUTER VIRUS THAT I'M GOING TO STICK ON THE INTERNET.

CHEEZOS

IT'S DESIGNED TO INFECT THE MACHINES OF USERS OF THE alt.government.-conspiracy.-paranoid NEWSGROUP.

CHEEZOS

AT A RANDOM DATE, THEIR SCREENS WILL GO BLACK, SPUTTER FOR A SECOND, THEN DISPLAY THE MESSAGE, "THEY ARE COMING."

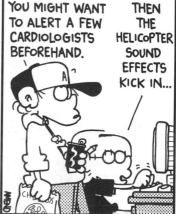
YOU MIGHT WANT TO ALERT A FEW CARDIOLOGISTS BEFOREHAND.

THEN THE HELICOPTER SOUND EFFECTS KICK IN...

CHEEZOS

AMEND

AAAA! WE'RE OUT OF COFFEE?! WE CAN'T BE! NOT TODAY!

I'VE GOT TO GIVE A PRESENTATION IN TWO HOURS! WE'RE OUT OF INSTANT, TOO?! AAAA!

I GOT THE LAST CUP, DAD, SORRY.

SINCE WHEN DID YOU TURN INTO MISTER MONEYBAGS?

LET'S SEE... I'LL HAVE FOUR DOUBLE HULKBURGERS...

I AM UNIQUE!

I AM SPECIAL!

I HAVE WORTH!

SO HOW COME ALL I SEE IS THAT ZIT ON MY CHIN?

AAAA! WHO RECORDED OVER MY "X-FILES" TAPE?! I GOT UP EXTRA EARLY JUST TO SEE IT! I'VE BEEN WAITING ALL WEEK FOR THIS!

SOMEONE IN THIS FAMILY IS A BONE-HEADED VCR MORON AND I INTEND TO FIND OUT WHO! HEADS WILL ROLL!

OH, WAIT — THIS ISN'T MY "X-FILES" TAPE. MINE MUST BE THIS OTHER ONE.

FALSE ALARM, PEOPLE — GO BACK TO SLEEP.

ONE YOUNG HEAD IS ABOUT TO ROLL...

FoxTrot
BILL AMEND

MOM! PAIGE IS TAKING THE LAST HO-HO!

IT'S **MINE**! I HAD DIBS!

MOM SAID I COULD HAVE IT IF I DID MY HOMEWORK, SO GIVE IT UP!

DIBS HAVE PRECEDENCE! ASK ANYBODY! LET GO!

LET'S SEE... WHAT WAS IT SOLOMON SUGGESTED UNDER THESE CIRCUMSTANCES?

SOMETHING ABOUT CUTTING KIDS IN HALF?

HERE, PAIGE, **YOU** TAKE IT.

NO, NO, I INSIST...

I'M JUST A HUNKA-HUNKA BURNIN' LOVE... WOOOO...

I'M JUST A HUNKA-HUNKA BURNIN' LOVE... OH, YEAH...

I'M JUST A HUNKA-HUNKA BURNIN' LOVE... YESSIR...

HUNKA-HUNKA-HUNKA BURNIN'-BURNIN'-BURNIN'...

JASON, DOWN IN THE BASEMENT, THERE'S A VALVE MARKED "COLD WATER SHUTOFF"...

I THOUGHT YOU'D NEVER ASK.

HEY, PAIGE, CHECK IT OUT— I MADE A SNOWMAN THAT LOOKS JUST LIKE YOU!

AND SO CONVENIENTLY IN THE MIDDLE OF THE STREET.

OH, LOOK— HERE COMES A PLOW...

PETER, I THOUGHT WE AGREED, NO "DONKEY KONG" UNTIL YOUR HOMEWORK IS DONE. MOM, MOM, MOM...

YOU MISUNDERSTOOD. WHAT I SAID WAS, NO HOMEWORK UNTIL "DONKEY KONG" IS DONE.

AND WHEN WILL **THAT** BE? BEST I CAN FIGURE, MID- TO LATE APRIL.

CARE TO EXPLAIN THESE SHARDS OF PLASTIC IN THE CARPET? YOU KNOW HOW, ON OCCASION, MOM HAS NO SENSE OF HUMOR?

I TELL YOU, NICOLE, WHEN THE CAFETERIA HAS PIZZA FOR LUNCH, IT'S LIKE ALL MY TROUBLES DISAPPEAR.

I MEAN, WHO **CARES** ABOUT A DUMB SHAKESPEARE QUIZ?! WHO **CARES** THAT I'VE GOT A LAB REPORT DUE?! WHO **CARES** THAT I LEFT MY BOOK BAG AT HOME?! I'M GOING TO HAVE **PIZZA**! WELL, I'D BETTER GO GET IN LINE.

DON'T YOU KEEP YOUR WALLET IN YOUR BOOK BAG?

YOU CAN HAVE MY YOGURT... THE IRONY GODS MUST BE ROLLING ON THE FLOOR.

WHAT ARE YOU DOING? AIMING MY SPEAKERS INTO THE FLOOR.

THIS WAY, I CAN LISTEN TO MY STEREO WHILE I'M DOWNSTAIRS DOING MY HOMEWORK IN THE DINING ROOM, WHICH HAPPENS TO BE RIGHT BENEATH US. NOW ALL I HAVE TO DO IS CRANK UP THE VOLUME.

WHAT'S THAT NOISE? THAT'S THE MUSIC. IT'S KINDA MUTED FROM THE CARPETING.

NO, IT SOUNDED MORE LIKE A CHANDELIER CRASHING. SAY, WERE THE PICTURES ON MY WALL ALWAYS THIS CROOKED?

84

FoxTrot
BILL AMEND

PETER, YOU DRANK THIS WHOLE POT OF COFFEE?! I NEED THE CAFFEINE FOR THIS MORNING'S MATH TEST.

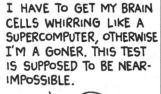

I HAVE TO GET MY BRAIN CELLS WHIRRING LIKE A SUPERCOMPUTER, OTHERWISE I'M A GONER. THIS TEST IS SUPPOSED TO BE NEAR-IMPOSSIBLE.

I FIGURE AFTER EIGHT CUPS I'M BOUND TO BE ONE LIGHTNING-FAST COMPUTATION MACHINE.

IF THE BOYS' BATHROOM IS 150 FEET AWAY AND I RUN AT A RATE OF 20 FEET PER SECOND... MR. FOX, IS THERE A REASON YOU KEEP SQUIRMING?

THEY CANCELED SCHOOL BECAUSE OF THE SNOW!

♪ THEY CANCELED SCHOOL! ♫ THEY CANCELED SCHOOL! ♪

♩ THEY—...

JUST WHO DO THEY THINK THEY ARE?! NICE TRY.

HEE HEE HEE... WHAT ARE YOU DOING?

MISTING MY SNOWBALLS WITH WATER SO THEY'LL TURN INTO ICEBALLS. I'M DECLARING ALL-OUT WAR ON PAIGE. HERE SHE COMES NOW.

HEY, PAIGE, YOU MANGY SEWER SPORE— I HOPE YOU'RE PRE-PARED FOR A PUMMELING!

HAVE FUN. UH-OH. OH, I AM READY, BELIEVE ME...

HI. I'D LIKE A SLICE OF PIZZA WITH PEPPERONI...

...MUSHROOMS... SAUSAGE... BLACK OLIVES... ONIONS... ARTICHOKE HEARTS... PEPPER-PEPPERONI...

YOU ALREADY SAID PEPPERONI.

I KNOW. I MEAN ANOTHER LAYER OF IT.

...ANCHOVIES... SAUSAGE... EXTRA CHEESE...

LUIGI, YOUR FAVORITE CUSTOMER IS BACK.

TELL HIM I'M STILL CLEANING THE OVEN FROM HIS LAST VISIT!

POTATO CHIPS... PRETZELS... HOT DOG BUNS...

WHAT ARE YOU DOING?

MAKING MY PRE-SUPER BOWL CHECKLIST.

I LIKE TO MAKE SURE I'VE GOT ALL THE SUPPLIES I'LL NEED AHEAD OF TIME. THAT WAY, I CAN AVOID A MAD DASH TO THE STORE ON SUNDAY. I RECOMMEND THIS FOR ANYONE.

ASPIRIN... ANTACID... EAR PLUGS...

HAVE YOU SEEN MY LUCKY ONE-GALLON BEER STEIN ANYWHERE?

CHECKMATE.

I WIN.

HA HA HA HA HA HA HA HA HA HA HA HA...

THE PROBLEM WITH LAPTOPS IS THERE'S NO PLUG TO RIP OUT OF THE WALL.

ANOTHER GAME, CHUMP-BOY?

FoxTrot
BILL AMEND

I **REALLY** DO NOT WANT TO GO TO WORK THIS WEEK.

WHY'S THAT?

PEMBROOK'S BRINGING IN SOME EFFICIENCY CONSULTANT TO TRY TO SQUEEZE EVEN MORE SAVINGS OUT OF MY DEPARTMENT. IT'S GOING TO BE A NIGHTMARE, I CAN TELL.

HAVE YOU MET THIS PERSON?

FRED DID. HE SAID SHE WAS SOME SORT OF BIGWIG.

WELL, THAT'S EXCITING. AT LEAST YOU KNOW SHE'LL HAVE SOME GOOD IDEAS.

NO, NO, I SAID SHE **WEARS** A BIG WIG. GREAT.

MEDIUM-TIP PENS?! DO YOU THINK INK GROWS ON TREES?!

MR. FOX, YOUR SUPERIORS BROUGHT ME IN THIS WEEK TO HELP INCREASE YOUR DEPARTMENT'S EFFICIENCY.

BUDGETS ARE TIGHT, AND WASTE WILL NO LONGER BE TOLERATED.

SO ENOUGH CHIT-CHAT. LET'S GET TO WORK.

ITEM ONE: THIS PERFECTLY GOOD PAPER CLIP I FOUND IN YOUR TRASH.

BARB, ANY CHANCE I'VE GOT A MEETING TO GO TO?

MR. FOX, WHAT'S THIS?!

UM, A PENCIL?

IT'S A Nº 2½ PENCIL, TO BE PRECISE. I FOUND IT ON YOUR DESK.

I LIKE Nº 2½ PENCILS. SO WHAT?

MR. FOX, I'VE CHECKED AND NO ONE ELSE IN THIS DEPARTMENT USES Nº 2½ PENCILS. EFFICIENCY DEMANDS THAT ALL PENCILS IN THIS OFFICE BE THE SAME AND PURCHASED IN BULK. YOUR LITTLE PENCIL INDULGENCE IS UNNECESSARILY COSTING THIS COMPANY PENNIES EACH MONTH. **PENNIES!**

LET'S PICK THIS UP LATER. YOUR BOSS IS TREATING ME TO LUNCH AT THE RITZ IN 10 MINUTES.

ABOUT YOUR "ONE PAPER CUP FOR THE WEEK" POLICY...

THE NAME OF THE GAME IN BUSINESS, MR. FOX, IS EFFICIENCY. WASTED TIME IS WASTED MONEY.

TAKE, FOR EXAMPLE, THE WAY YOU ARE WALKING THROUGH THIS OFFICE: LEFT TURNS, RIGHT TURNS, UP THE STAIRS, DOWN THE STAIRS.

IF YOU JUST STOPPED WEAVING ALL OVER THE PLACE, YOU'D GET WHEREVER YOU'RE GOING IN HALF THE TIME!

NOW, TELL ME, **WHAT** IS IT THAT YOU'RE TRYING TO GET **TO**?

THE QUESTION SHOULD BE **WHO** AM I TRYING TO GET AWAY **FROM**.

WHAT **IS** THIS?!

THE CENTERPIECE OF MY EFFICIENCY REVIEW.

I'VE NOTICED THAT WHEN YOU AND YOUR STAFF WORK ON THE COMPUTER, YOUR LEGS ARE UNOCCUPIED. IF WE COULD TRAIN YOUR PEOPLE TO TYPE WITH THEIR FEET ON A SECOND KEYBOARD, WE COULD LAY OFF HALF YOUR STAFF WITH NO LOSS IN PRODUCTIVITY.

OF COURSE, IF WE DOUBLE PEOPLES' WORKLOADS, WE'D PROBABLY HAVE TO GIVE THEM 10 PERCENT RAISES...

WHY DO I KEEP THINKING TODAY IS APRIL 1?

YOU KNOW, MY LAST CLIENT'S EYE HAD THAT EXACT SAME TWITCH.

WELL, MR. FOX, I'VE FINISHED MY REPORT ON WAYS TO MAKE YOUR DEPARTMENT MORE EFFICIENT.

BY MY BEST ESTIMATION, THE CHANGES I SUGGEST YOU IMPLEMENT WILL SAVE THIS OFFICE OVER $1,000 EACH YEAR.

WOW. THAT'S GREAT.

...LESS, OF COURSE, MY FEE FOR THIS PAST WEEK.

PLEASE TELL ME YOU FORGOT THE DECIMAL POINT.

LOOK, 11½ YEARS FROM NOW YOUR COMPANY WILL THANK ME.

FoxTrot
BILL AMEND

MOM! MOM! I GOT A 91 PERCENT ON MY MATH TEST!

WHY, PAIGE, THAT'S GREAT!

IT'S THE BEST I'VE DONE ON A MATH TEST ALL YEAR! IT BRINGS MY AVERAGE UP TO A STRAIGHT "B"!

SEE WHAT HAPPENS WHEN YOU STUDY?

I'M IN SUCH A GOOD MOOD! NOTHING COULD DEPRESS ME RIGHT NOW!

MOM! MOM! I GOT A 108 PERCENT ON MY MATH TEST!

I ALWAYS SPEAK TOO SOON.

WHY, JASON, THAT'S GREAT!

IT'S A NEW SCHOOL RECORD!

O GREAT OUIJA BOARD...

PLEASE GRANT ME AN ANSWER TO THIS QUESTION...

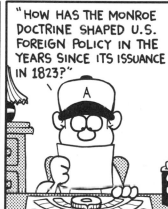

"HOW HAS THE MONROE DOCTRINE SHAPED U.S. FOREIGN POLICY IN THE YEARS SINCE ITS ISSUANCE IN 1823?"

I FIGURE IT'S WORTH A SHOT.

PETER, WILL YOU JUST WRITE YOUR STUPID ESSAY?!

```
fontSize:= 36;
FOR i:= 1 to 1000 DO
  BEGIN
    writeln ('KICK ME');
    writeln;
  END;
```

PRINTZZZ...
PRINTZZZ...
PRINTZZZ...
PRINTZZZ...

YOU GOTTA LOVE THE PERSON WHO INVENTED FORM-FEED LABELS.

HIYA, TRACY. NICE JOB ON THAT REPORT LAST MONTH!

PAT PAT

BLINK
BLINK
BLINK

ZZZZZ...

WHUMP!

I'VE REALLY GOT TO STOP NODDING OFF IN ART CLASS.

I JUST CAN'T FIGURE OUT THIS CREDIT CARD STATEMENT.

IN WHAT WAY?

IT'S BIZARRE. IT SHOWS A PURCHASE, THEN A CREDIT, THEN A PURCHASE, THEN A CREDIT, THEN A PURCHASE, THEN A CREDIT...

WHAT'S GOING ON?? IS IT A COMPUTER GLITCH?

DAD, THINK ABOUT IT.

MOM, **PLEASE** DON'T MAKE ME TAKE THIS BACK!

PAIGE, THAT SWEATER COST MORE THAN MY COLLEGE TUITION!

MUNCH
MUNCH
MUNCH
MUNCH

YOU KNOW... WHAT ARE CHOCOLATE CHIP COOKIES WITHOUT A GLASS OF MILK?

GLUG
GLUG
GLUG
GLUG

YOU KNOW... WHAT'S A GLASS OF MILK WITHOUT A FEW CHOCOLATE CHIP COOKIES?...

AÂÂÂAA!

SCARY NOVEL?

ITTY-BITTY PRINTING.

HEY, PAIGE, I DIDN'T KNOW YOU AND JANE GOODALL WERE BUDDIES!

WHAT ARE YOU TALKING ABOUT?

THIS MAGAZINE HAS A PICTURE OF YOU TWO STANDING ARM-IN-ARM IN THE JUNGLE.

SHE HAS HER ARM AROUND A CHIMPANZEE!

OH. WHOOPS. MY MISTAKE.

THAT IS SO MEAN! GIVE ME THAT!

HEY, PETER, I DIDN'T KNOW YOU AND JANE GOODALL WERE BUDDIES!

WHAT ARE YOU TALKING ABOUT?

OK, MY PRETTY VALENTINE, NOW CLOSE YOUR EYES...

YOU GOT ME FLOWERS?!

NO...

CHOCOLATES?!

NO...

JEWELRY?!?

ANDY, GEEZ! YOU'VE BEEN WANTING A NEW SPATULA FOR YEARS!

EVER WONDER, ROGER, WHY NONE OF OUR KIDS HAVE BIRTHDAYS IN NOVEMBER?

BOING!

BOING!

BOING!

BOING!

NOPE. THE SPIDER'S STILL UP THERE.

MAYBE WE SHOULD GET A BIGGER SUPERBALL...

PAIGE, QUIT HOGGING THE POPCORN!

THERE'S PLENTY! CALM DOWN, YOU SPAZ!

YOU'VE EATEN HALF THE BOWL! LET ME HOLD IT FOR A CHANGE!

I'M THE ONE WHO MADE IT! LEGGO!

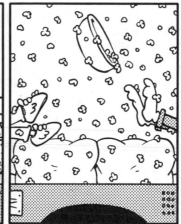

WHEN YOU FACTOR IN THE THREE HOURS OF CLEANING, I'M NOT SURE RENTING MOVIES IS ALL THAT GREAT A BARGAIN.

JASON, QUIT HOGGING THE ICE CREAM!

MOM, THE CEILING'S DRIPPING!

THAT'S ODD, THE ONLY THING ABOVE YOU IS PAIGE'S BEDROOM.

I STILL CAN'T BELIEVE HUNKY JIMMY ANDREWS IS MOVING!

WA-AA!

FoxTrot
BILL AMEND

JASON AND PETER ARE AT THE DENTIST... MOM'S RUNNING ERRANDS... DAD'S STILL AT WORK...

I CAN'T BELIEVE I'VE GOT THE ENTIRE HOUSE TO MYSELF! WEEEEEEEEEEE!

WHAT TIME DID THEY SAY THEY'D GET BACK?...

QUINCY, SHOO!

I MEAN IT! SHOO!

I'M TRYING TO READ! SHOO! SHOO! SHOO! SHOO! SHOO! SHOO! **SHOO!**

HAS JASON TAUGHT YOU **NOTHING?!**

QUINCY, WILL YOU STOP EATING MY SHOELACE?!

OK, FINE. SWALLOW THE SHOELACE. SEE WHAT **I** CARE. YOU'LL PROBABLY CHOKE TO DEATH ON IT.

Hack! Hack! Gack!

WHY CAN'T I EVER BE THIS RIGHT WHEN IT COMES TO THINGS LIKE SCHOOLWORK?

LOOK AT THIS, QUINCY! YOU'VE GOT THE ENTIRE SHOELACE STUCK IN YOUR THROAT!

OK, IT'S OUT. YOU CAN BREATHE NOW. QUINCY? I SAID YOU CAN BREATHE NOW.

LET ME PUT IT THIS WAY, QUINCY—IT'S GROSS ENOUGH THAT I'M SITTING HERE HOLDING AN IGUANA...

...I'M NOT ABOUT TO BE HOLDING A **DEAD** ONE!

Gasp!
Gasp!
Cough!
Gasp!
Gasp!

WELL, QUINCY, YOU'VE MADE THIS QUITE THE INTERESTING AFTERNOON.

I JUST HOPE YOU'VE LEARNED YOUR LESSON.

THAT IS, IF YOU WANT TO LIVE, DON'T GO CHEWING ON SHOELACES.

I SHOULD WARN YOU, THE SAME GOES FOR CERTAIN NOSES.

JASON'S GONNA FREAK WHEN I TELL HIM I SAVED YOU FROM CHOKING.

I MEAN, I'M GONNA **OWN** THAT BOY! HE'LL DEDICATE HIS WHOLE **LIFE** TO THANKING ME!

...OF COURSE, THAT PROBABLY MEANS HE'LL SPEND IT FOLLOWING ME AROUND...

ON SECOND THOUGHT, LET'S JUST KEEP THIS OUR LITTLE SECRET.

FoxTrot
BILL AMEND

Panel 1: WHAT'S THE WEATHER SUPPOSED TO BE LIKE TODAY? / LET'S SEE...

Panel 2: RAIN. LOTS OF IT. UP TO 10 INCHES EXPECTED. / Cartoonist Charms at White House Gala

Panel 3: GREAT. / ALL DAY LONG. RAIN, RAIN, RAIN, RAIN, RAIN...

Panel 4: ...IN GUATEMALA. / FIGURES THIS HAPPENS ON CLASS-PHOTO DAY.

Panel 5: WHAT ARE YOU DOING? / MAILING FAN LETTERS TO MYSELF.

Panel 6: THIS WAY, WHEN I REALLY **DO** BECOME HUGELY IMPORTANT AND FAMOUS, I'LL BE USED TO THE ADULATION AND IT WON'T MESS WITH MY HEAD. I'D HATE FOR MY EGO TO GO BONKERS.

Panel 7: OF COURSE, THE MERE FACT THAT I'M DOING THIS MEANS IT'S PROBABLY TOO LATE.

Panel 8: I THINK "GOD-LIKE" IS TWO WORDS. / HI, I'D LIKE TO CANCEL ALL THOSE FLOWERS I ORDERED...

Panel 9: SEE, THE HIGHLANDER IS AN IMMORTAL, WHICH MEANS HE CAN'T BE KILLED. / UH-HUH.

Panel 10: ...UNLESS HE GETS HIS HEAD CHOPPED OFF, WHICH IS WHY THEY ALL CARRY SWORDS UNDER THEIR COATS. / AND YOU ACTUALLY **WATCH** THIS SHOW?!

Panel 11: WHAT? — IT'S COOL! / JASON, THAT IS THE MOST RIDICULOUS AND UNBELIEVABLE PREMISE FOR A TV SHOW THAT I'VE EVER HEARD OF! I CAN'T BELIEVE YOU BUY INTO THIS NONSENSE!

Panel 12: SEE, BILLY AND ALLISON WERE **GOING** TO GET MARRIED, BUT THEN BILLY MARRIED BROOKE AND ALLISON MARRIED BROOKE'S DAD. / UH-HUH.

STEVE'S DAD SET UP THIS AMAZING HOME THEATER IN THEIR BASEMENT.

THEY'VE NOW GOT THIS BIG-SCREEN TV WITH FIVE-FOOT SPEAKERS ON EITHER SIDE, THX SURROUND SOUND AND THIS KILLER 200-WATT SUB-WOOFER. HE SHOWED THIS ONE SCENE FROM "JURASSIC PARK" AND I SWEAR, I THOUGHT WE WERE ACTUALLY GOING TO DIE, WHAT WITH ALL THE SHAKING.

THE DINOSAURS SEEMED THAT REAL?

NO, NO, I THOUGHT THE HOUSE WAS GOING TO COLLAPSE ON TOP OF US.

AND TO THINK I WASTED MY CHILDHOOD WATCHING MOVIES THAT EMPHASIZED PLOT.

STEVE SAYS WITH "DIE HARD III," YOU CAN SEE THEIR WINDOWS FLEX.

AMEND

THEY LOOK LIKE THEY FIT OK. HOW DO THEY FEEL?

NOT BAD. LET ME TEST THEM OUT.

SAY "HERE COMES YOUR SISTER IN NOTHING BUT HER UNDERWEAR."

AMEND

HERE COMES YOUR SISTER IN NOTHING BUT HER UNDERWEAR.

AIEEE!

YOU KNOW, I THINK I'VE SOLD YOU SHOES BEFORE.

DO YOU HAVE ANYTHING WITH A LITTLE MORE TRACTION?

AMEND

IF YOU THINK I'M GONNA FEEL GUILTY ABOUT ENJOYING THIS WEATHER...

FoxTrot
BILL AMEND

THE COMPUTER ATE MY COLUMN...

THE REFRIGERATOR LEAKED WATER ALL OVER THE KITCHEN...

THE CITY DECIDED OUR STREET WAS IN DESPERATE NEED OF JACKHAMMERING...

COULD A DAY STINK ANY WORSE?

MIND IF I LIGHT THIS BABY UP BEFORE DINNER?

ROGER, WHAT IS THAT THING IN YOUR MOUTH?!

IT'S A CIGAR.

I KNOW THAT. WHAT ARE YOU DOING WITH IT?

FRED GAVE IT TO ME.

CHECK OUT THE FANCY LABEL: AROMA DEL BAÑO.

ROGER, DID YOU EVER STUDY SPANISH IN SCHOOL?

MY PRONUNCIATION IS THAT GOOD, EH?

ROGER, I DON'T WANT THAT THING IN MY HOUSE.

ANDY, WHERE HAVE YOU BEEN? CIGARS ARE VERY HIP RIGHT NOW.

ROGER, I MEAN IT.

ALL THE YOUNG GUYS AT WORK ARE SMOKING THEM!

YOU'RE NOT ONE OF THEM.

IT'S THE STYLE! IT'S THE TREND! IT'S THE RAGE!

YOU GOT THE "RAGE" PART RIGHT.

ANDY, C'MON— LET ME BACK IN...

FoxTrot
BILL AMEND

ICK. PEANUT BUTTER.

I CAN'T BELIEVE YOU AND I HAVE BEEN GOING OUT FOR OVER A YEAR NOW, DENISE.

403 DAYS.

SERIOUSLY, WHODATHUNKIT?

I MEAN, YOU'RE SMART AND FUNNY AND PRETTY AND WONDERFUL AND FRIENDLY AND THOUGHTFUL AND PERFECT AND WHAT AM I?!

PERCEPTIVE?

BY THE WAY, YOU'VE GOT SOME QUALITIES THAT I DIDN'T MENTION...

PETER, I THOUGHT MAYBE YOU COULD COME OVER AFTER DINNER TONIGHT.

SURE. JUST TO HANG OUT?

WELL, ACTUALLY, YOU SEE, MY PARENTS ARE GOING TO BE OUT AND I WAS HOPING WE COULD, UM...YOU KNOW...

GEEZ, I FEEL LIKE SUCH A GEEK SAYING THIS...

I THINK I CAN GUESS WHAT YOU HAVE IN MIND.

I WANT TO STUDY FOR NEXT MONTH'S SATs.

THE ONE TEEN-AGER IN THE UNIVERSE WITH A WORK ETHIC AND SHE HAS TO BE MY GIRLFRIEND.

"MNEMONIC," PETER— WHAT'S IT MEAN?

SO, DENISE, WHAT TIME DID YOUR PARENTS SAY THEY'D BE BACK?

"ASPERSION," PETER— WHAT'S IT MEAN?

I MEAN, WAS IT SOON? LATER? LOTS LATER?...

"ISOMORPHISM," PETER— WHAT'S IT MEAN?

...BECAUSE IF IT WAS LOTS LATER, WE'D HAVE TIME TO STUDY AND TO...

"SELF-CONTROL," PETER— WHAT'S IT MEAN?

EASY FOR YOU TO SAY— YOU DON'T HAVE TO LOOK AT ME.

LOOK, PETER, MY HORMONES ARE JUST AS ACTIVE AS YOURS ARE — IF NOT MORE SO — BUT THAT'S NOT THE ISSUE HERE.

THE POINT IS, WHEN I ASKED MY PARENTS IF YOU COULD COME OVER AND HELP ME STUDY, I HAD TO PROMISE THEM THAT THIS WOULDN'T TURN INTO ONE OF OUR USUAL KISSFESTS. I TOLD YOU THAT BEFORE YOU GOT HERE.

SO NO SMOOCHING. I GAVE MY WORD. SORRY.

WHAT ABOUT PLAIN OL' GROPING?

PETER, I REALLY HOPE YOU'RE SMILING RIGHT NOW.

DENISE? WE'RE HOME.

OH, HI, DAD. PETER AND I ARE IN THE DEN.

WE'LL LEAVE YOU KIDS ALONE, THEN. HOW'D YOUR STUDYING GO?

PRETTY WELL. JUST A FEW THINGS LEFT TO DO.

SMACK!

MMPH!

I ONLY PROMISED THEM I WOULDN'T KISS YOU WHILE THEY WERE GONE.

AIR... GASP... AIR... GASP...

YOU KNOW, DENISE, I REALLY WISH I HAD YOUR WILLPOWER.

I TOTALLY WAS MR. HORMONES TONIGHT. IT WAS LIKE I COULDN'T EVEN THINK ABOUT STUDYING! I FEEL LIKE SUCH A LOSER.

I WISH I HAD YOUR WILL-POWER... I WISH I HAD YOUR SELF-CONTROL... I WISH I HAD YOUR WORK ETHIC AND INTEGRITY AND ALL THOSE THINGS I DON'T HAVE.

BUT YOU DO HAVE THEM, IN A WAY.

...YOU HAVE ME.

WHAT CONCERNS ME, THOUGH, IS THAT YOU'VE GOT ME.

FoxTrot
BILL AMEND

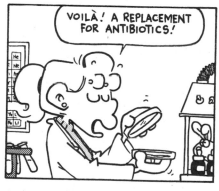

WHERE'S PAIGE? I HAVEN'T SEEN HER ALL AFTER-NOON.

SHE AND NICOLE WENT TO THE LIBRARY. I THINK THEY'RE RESEARCHING COLLEGES.

COLLEGES?

YOU KNOW, TRYING TO FIGURE OUT WHICH ONES THEY WANT TO APPLY TO.

(SNIFF) OH, PETER...A MOTHER LIVES FOR MOMENTS LIKE THIS. MY LITTLE GIRL HAS FINALLY DECIDED TO TAKE ACADEMICS SERIOUSLY.

ICK. NOTRE DAME'S COLORS TOTALLY CLASH WITH MY SKIN TONE.

STANFORD'S RED WOULD GO GREAT WITH THOSE CUTE SHOES YOU BOUGHT.

I COMMAND THIS RAIN TO STOP!

I COMMAND THIS RAIN TO STOP!

I COMMAND THIS RAIN TO –...

SOME PROOFS OF OMNIPOTENCE ARE INEVITABLE.

WHERE HAVE YOU BEEN FOR THE LAST SIX HOURS?

LET'S HOPE THEY NEVER PUT MY SISTER'S IMAGE ON A COIN.

WHY'S THAT?

THERE'D BE NO WAY TO TELL THE HEAD FROM THE TAIL!

WAAA HA HA HAR HEE HEE!

OH, MAN, PAIGE WOULD KILL ME IF SHE EVER HEARD THAT.

WHAT DO YOU MEAN SHE'S NOT HOME?!

UM, PAIGE, I WAS SICK YESTERDAY AND I WAS WONDERING...

...UM, WAS WONDERING WHAT CHAPTERS WE WERE SUPPOSED TO...

...UM... SUPPOSED... TO... UM...

I KNEW IT WAS A MISTAKE TO EAT SOUR PATCH KIDS AT SCHOOL.

SO, UM, ARE YOU BUSY FRIDAY NIGHT?

SLURRRP...

P.P.PAIGE, AB·B·BOUT THIS COFFEE YOU M·M·MADE...

I ALWAYS FORGET— IS IT A TEASPOON OF GROUND COFFEE FOR EACH CUP OF WATER, OR VICE VERSA?

WHAT ARE YOU DOING?

MODIFYING THIS VIDEO GAME.

DOOMATHON HAS THIS UTILITY PROGRAM THAT LETS YOU CREATE YOUR OWN MONSTERS AND WEAPONS. CHECK OUT THIS HEAT-SEEKING BAZOOKA I DESIGNED.

AND CHECK OUT THE CREATURES I'LL BE USING IT ON...

I SEE YOU'VE WISELY MADE ABOUT 25 BACK-UP COPIES.

PAIGE'S YEARBOOK PHOTO WAS BLACK AND WHITE, SO THE GREEN MAY BE A LITTLE OFF...

FoxTrot
BILL AMEND

FAUNTLEROY, LET GO OF MY LEG!

Grrrrrr

I MEAN IT! LET GO!

Grrrrr Grrrrr

LISTEN, YOU PSYCHOTIC LITTLE RAT-DOG, IF YOU DON'T STOP CHEWING ON MY LEG THIS INSTANT, I'M GOING TO PUNT YOU LIKE A BONY LITTLE FOOTBALL INTO GOD KNOWS WHAT TIME ZONE!

OK, SO TECHNICALLY YOU DID OBEY ME...

Grrrrr

YES, FAUNTLEROY, IT'S ANOTHER DOG.

YIP! YIP! YIP! YIP! YIP! YIP!

YES, FAUNTLEROY, HE'S WITH-IN 50 MILES OF YOUR HOUSE.

YIP! YIP! YIP! YIP! YIP! YIP! YIP! YIP! YIP! YIP!

YES, FAUNTLEROY, YOU HAVE EVERY RIGHT TO TELL HIM TO SCRAM.

YIP! YIP! YIP! YIP! YIP! YIP! YIP!

I'M GUESSING, FAUNTLEROY, THAT YOUR ANCESTORS MUST HAVE PROCREATED VERY, VERY QUICKLY.

YIP! YIP! YIP! YIP!

MRS. TAFT WANTS TO KNOW IF YOU AND FAUNTLEROY HAD FUN THIS WEEK.

DID WE HAVE FUN?!

EVERY TIME I WENT OVER THERE, THAT STUPID LITTLE PIRANHA-DOG SUNK HIS FANGS INTO MY LEGS! WHY DO YOU THINK I'VE BEEN LIMPING?! HE SHREDDED MY PANTS... HE CHEWED UP MY SOCKS...

AND DID I TELL YOU WHAT UNSPEAKABLE THING HE DID TO MY SNEAKERS ON THURSDAY?!

FOR WHAT IT'S WORTH, MRS. TAFT, I'VE HAD FUN THIS WEEK.

I MEAN, THESE USED TO BE WHITE!

FoxTrot
BILL AMEND

TAP TAP
TAP TAP
TAP TAP
TAP...

BEEP BEEP
BEEP BEEP
BEEP BEEP
BEEP...

Welcome to the Jason Fox World Wide Web Home Page!!!

- To view a photo of Jason, click here.

This is me, Jason Fox. I like science, math and Plasma Man comic books.

- To view a photo of my iguana, click here.

This is Quincy, my iguana. He likes to escape from his cage and eat things.

- To view a photo of my friend Marcus, click here.

This is my best friend, Marcus. He's pretty cool. We're a lot alike.

- To view a photo of my Saturn V model, click here.

This is the Saturn V rocket I built. Marcus wants to put his hamster on board.

- To view a photo of my sister Paige, click here.

IN ACCORDANCE WITH THE INDECENCY STATUTES OF THE 1996 FEDERAL TELECOMMUNICATIONS ACT, THE IMAGE OF MY SISTER'S OBSCENELY UGLY FACE IS NO LONGER AVAILABLE FOR PUBLIC VIEWING AT THIS SITE.

- For the next best thing, click here.

METHINKS THE WEB HAS GOTTEN JUST A WEE TOO ACCESSIBLE.

WHY'S IT NOW LINKING ME TO THE COLUMBUS ZOO CHIMP FACILITY?

NOW, MOM, DON'T FREAK OUT, BUT SOME GUYS ON THE BASE-BALL TEAM LOST A BET WITH SOME GUYS ON THE SOCCER TEAM, AND...

WELL...

YOU SHAVED YOUR HEAD? HOW CUTE.

HEY, PAIGE, WE WERE WRONG— SHE DIDN'T GO BALLISTIC.

NOW TAKE OFF THAT SILLY BALD WIG AND GET READY FOR DINNER.

YOU MEAN THIS **WASN'T** AN APRIL FOOL'S JOKE?!

YOU REALLY **DID** SHAVE YOUR HEAD?!

AAAA! MY BEAUTIFUL SON! YOU LOOK LIKE A SKINHEAD!

PEOPLE WILL THINK YOU'RE A NAZI!

MICHAEL JORDAN HAS A SHAVED HEAD AND NO ONE CALLS **HIM** A NAZI...

PETER, HOW COULD YOU **DO** THIS?!

HOW COULD YOU AND YOUR FRIENDS MAKE SUCH A STUPID BET?!

WHAT ON EARTH WERE YOU THINKING?!

IT'S A PUZZLEMENT.

YOUR FATHER'S GOING TO LOVE THIS.

SO THE SOCCER TEAM DID THIS TO YOU AND YOUR BASEBALL TEAMMATES.

UM, YEAH.

BECAUSE YOU LOST SOME STUPID BET ABOUT WHO COULD EAT THE MOST TRIPLE BURGERS IN AN HOUR.

BASIC-ALLY.

SON, I'M GOING TO SAY SOMETHING THAT MAY SOUND A LITTLE INSENSITIVE, BUT...

I'M NOT THE BALDEST GUY IN THIS HOUSE ANYMORE! YEE-HA!

YOU KNOW, I THINK I'LL GO LET MOM CHEW ME OUT SOME MORE.

JASON, I SAID NO.

PLEEEEASE??

No!

PLEASE? PLEASE? PLEASE? PLEASE? PLEASE? PLEASE? PLEASE? PLEASE? PLEASE? PLEASE? PLEASE? PLEASE?

OK, FINE. BUT JUST THIS ONE TIME!

AHEAD, WARP FACTOR SEVEN. ENGAGE.

GOOSE BUMPS.

CHECK OUT ALL MY PEACH FUZZ!

AND THIS IS ONLY SINCE MONDAY!

I'LL BET IN ANOTHER WEEK OR TWO, I'LL SIMPLY LOOK LIKE A KID WITH A CREW CUT!

ISN'T IT GREAT THE WAY HAIR JUST GROWS RIGHT BACK?

LOOK, I'M SORRY I MADE FUN OF YOU, OK?!

FoxTrot
BILL AMEND

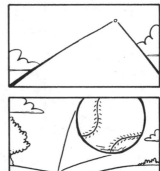

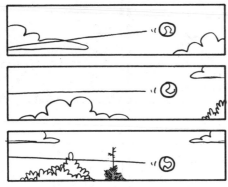

YOU KNOW, THAT WOULD HAVE BEEN PRETTY IMPRESSIVE HAD I ACTUALLY BEEN AIMING FOR THAT CAN.

SON, WHY DON'T WE LAY OFF THE KNUCKLEBALLS FOR A WHILE.

DON'T MOST PITCHERS AT LEAST HIT THE BACKSTOP?

MOM, DO YOU REMEMBER THAT "BRADY BUNCH" EPISODE WHERE PETER BUILDS A VOLCANO OUT ON THEIR BACK PATIO?

SORT OF.

THEY SHOW IT ALL THE TIME — YOU KNOW, WHERE IT BLOWS UP AND MUDDY GOOP GOES FLYING ALL OVER HIS SISTER AND IT'S REALLY FUNNY?

WOULD IT BE OK WITH YOU IF I DID SOMETHING LIKE THAT?

YOU WANT TO BUILD A VOLCANO TO HURL GOOP AT YOUR SISTER?

ACTUALLY, I PLANNED TO SKIP THE "VOLCANO" PART...

JASON, WHAT'S IN THAT BUCKET?

IS THIS BLOUSE WHITE OR WHAT?

ROGER, THERE'S A MR. STARK HERE TO SEE YOU.

OH, MAN! NOT ANOTHER SALES PITCH!

WHY CAN'T THESE SALESMEN LEAVE ME ALONE?! WHY CAN'T THEY SEE THAT I'M BUSY?! WHY CAN'T THEY COME AROUND ONCE A YEAR INSTEAD OF EVERY OTHER DAY?! WHY?!

... AND WHY CAN'T I EVER SAY NO?

ROGER, ROGER! YOU'RE GIVING ME WRITER'S CRAMP!

YOUR "DARK FORCES" CD-ROM WAS IN MY AEROSMITH CASE.

THAT MIGHT EXPLAIN WHY THESE ALIENS LOOK SO FUNNY.

FoxTrot
BILL AMEND

EXCUSE ME, BUT I THINK THE SLIDE IS UPSIDE-DOWN.

OH, VERY FUNNY.

TYRANNOSAURUS REX. TYRANT LIZARD. KING OF THE DINOSAURS.

BUT WAS HE REALLY KING? WAS HE REALLY THE MOST POWERFUL AND FEARED OF THE DINOSAURS? NEXT SLIDE, PLEASE.

IT IS MY CONTENTION THAT THE PLANT-EATING PACHYCEPHALOSAURUS WAS, IN FACT, THE TRUE KING OF THE LATE CRETACEOUS. HOW IS THIS POSSIBLE, YOU ASK?

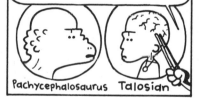

A COMPARISON OF ITS HEAD WITH THOSE OF THE TELEPATHIC TALOSIANS FEATURED IN STAR TREK'S "THE CAGE" EPISODE SUGGESTS STRONGLY THAT THESE CREATURES POSSESSED EXTRAORDINARY PSYCHIC ABILITIES.

Pachycephalosaurus   Talosian

TYRANNOSAURS, VELOCIRAPTORS AND OTHER PREDATORS MORE THAN LIKELY WERE TURNED INTO "THOUGHT SLAVES" BY THESE ALL-POWERFUL PACHYS... GIANT, MEAT-EATING PUPPETS READY TO OBEY THEIR MASTERS' EVERY WHIM.

Psychic waves

NOW, THEN, WHY DID DINOSAURS EVENTUALLY GO EXTINCT? MY THEORY: TIME-TRAVELING BIG-GAME HUNTERS. MY EVIDENCE? NEXT SLIDE.

GOT ONE!

AMEND

I STILL CAN'T BELIEVE THAT GUY AT THE SMITHSONIAN HUNG UP ON YOU.

I'M CRUSHING THEIR ORTHODOXY. WHAT DO YOU EXPECT?

THIS LETTER YOU SENT TO STEPHEN JAY GOULD SURE CAME BACK IN A HURRY.

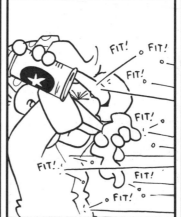

HOW'S THE BASEMENT CLEANING COMING ALONG?

WELL, I NEED SOME CLARIFICATION.

OH?

I NEED TO KNOW WHETHER YOU WANT IT SUPER CLEAN, PRETTY CLEAN OR JUST KINDA CLEAN. I'D HATE TO DO MORE WORK THAN I HAVE TO, IF YOU KNOW WHAT I MEAN.

WHAT HAVE YOU DONE SO FAR?

WELL, I, UM, TURNED ON THE LIGHT SWITCH...

KEEP GOING.

SLAVE DRIVER.

WHAT'S WITH THE GLEEFUL GIGGLING?

MOM ASKED ME TO BAG UP ANY CLOTHES I DON'T WANT SO SHE CAN GIVE THEM TO CHARITY.

SO?

SO I'M BAGGING UP ALL OF MY CLOTHES. THIS WAY, I WON'T HAVE ANYTHING TO WEAR TO SCHOOL ON MONDAY AND MOM WILL BE FORCED TO LET ME GO ON A MAJOR-LEAGUE SHOPPING SPREE.

EITHER THAT OR I'LL GET TO STAY HOME...

THIS I HADN'T COUNTED ON.

NICE OUTFIT.

MOMS DO IT IN MINI-VANS

WELL, I CLEANED THE HOUSE AND GARAGE, YOUR FATHER EMPTIED THE ATTIC...

YOUR BROTHER ORGANIZED THE BASEMENT, YOUR SISTER WEEDED ALL THE FLOWER BEDS...

AND YOU, PETER, THROUGHOUT THIS WHOLE WEEK, HAVE DONE ABSOLUTELY NOTHING. WHAT DO YOU HAVE TO SAY FOR YOURSELF?

WELL DONE, OL' BEAN?

LET'S REVIEW THE CHEMICALS IN THIS SQUIRT BOTTLE, SHALL WE?

PAT PAT

FoxTrot
BILL AMEND

HEY, PETER, LOOK WHAT I FOUND IN THE BASEMENT!

OH, YEAH— THAT'S MY OLD MAGIC SET.

I GOT IT FOR MY BIRTHDAY ABOUT FIVE YEARS AGO. I NEVER REALLY USED IT MUCH.

IF YOU DON'T WANT IT, CAN I HAVE IT?

SURE. WHY NOT?

WELL, JASON, YOU'VE CERTAINLY ANSWERED MY QUESTION.

C'MON—IT'LL JUST LOOK LIKE I'M CHOPPING OFF YOUR FINGERS...

I FIGURED OUT WHAT I'M GOING TO DO FOR A LIVING.

OH?

I'M GOING TO BE THE WORLD'S GREATEST MAGICIAN! I'LL DO TV SPECIALS! LIVE SHOWS! I'LL FILL STADIUMS! WHAT A LIFE!

DID YOU KNOW THAT DAVID COPPERFIELD MAKES AN EIGHT-FIGURE INCOME?

OF COURSE, HE ALSO HAS SUPERMODELS THROWING THEMSELVES AT HIM.

I SUPPOSE THERE ARE DOWNSIDES TO EVERYTHING.

WHY THE LONG FACE?

PETER GAVE ME HIS OLD MAGIC SET, BUT ALL THE TRICKS IN IT ARE REALLY LAME.

LOOK AT THIS JUNK — CUPS AND BALLS... SPONGE RABBITS... A HANDKERCHIEF THAT CHANGES COLOR... THEY CALL THIS **MAGIC**?!

WHERE'S THE FIRE?! WHERE ARE THE TIGERS?! WHERE'S THE BED OF SPEARS I CAN DANGLE MYSELF OVER WHILE I TRY TO GET OUT OF LEG IRONS?!

DEAR, I TAKE BACK ALL THOSE JOKES ABOUT YOUR HAIR GOING GRAY.

WHAT I REALLY NEED IS A GOOD STRAIT-JACKET.

FLIP FLIP FLIP

SOMEHOW I EXPECTED MORE BARGAINING WITH THE DEVIL AND FEWER WIRES AND MIRRORS.

ONLY **YOU** WOULD SEEM DISAPPOINTED BY THIS.

WANT TO SEE MY DEATH-DEFYING STRAITJACKET ESCAPE? I'VE BEEN PRACTICING IT ALL AFTERNOON.

SURE.

OOF... UGGH... ALMOST THERE... OOF... HERE WE GO...

TA DA!

WHERE'S THE DEFYING-DEATH PART?

THAT'LL COME WHEN PAIGE SEES WHAT THIS HAS DONE TO HER SWEATER.

HAVE YOU CONSIDERED WORKING UP A GOOD VANISHING ACT?

AND NOW, THE MOMENT YOU'VE ALL BEEN WAITING FOR! I REACH INTO MY HAT AND PRODUCE NOT **ONE**, BUT —...

UM...

SHOOT— WHERE'D THEY ALL GO?

WHERE'D WHAT ALL GO?

WELL, MARCUS, I FIGURED OUT WHY MAGICIANS DON'T TYPICALLY WORK WITH SNAKES...

FoxTrot
BILL AMEND

Tweeee!

I SWEAR, EVERYONE'S A CRITIC.

OK, EVERYONE, HOLD ON TO YOUR SEATS!...

...BECAUSE YOU ARE ABOUT TO EXPERIENCE A NEW TASTE SENSATION KNOWN AS EGGS À LA PAIGE!

NOT FRIED... NOT SCRAMBLED... BUT SOMEWHERE DELIGHTFULLY IN BETWEEN.

WITH A DELICATE CHEESE TOPPING AND BIG HUNKS OF BEEF THROUGHOUT.

ACTUALLY, ALL OUR BEEF WAS FROZEN, SO I USED BOUILLON CUBES INSTEAD.

I'VE ALSO WHIPPED UP A BATCH OF ORANGE JUICE À LA PAIGE.

THEY NEVER HOLD ON TO THEIR SEATS.

AMEND

127